AUTHORS AND OTHERS

AUTHORS AND OTHERS

BY

ANICE PAGE COOPER

Essay Index Reprint Series

originally published by

DOUBLEDAY, PAGE & COMPANY

BOOKS FOR LIBRARIES PRESS
FREEPORT, NEW YORK

First Published 1927
Reprinted 1970

STANDARD BOOK NUMBER:
8369-1493-7

LIBRARY OF CONGRESS CATALOG CARD NUMBER.
70-107689

PRINTED IN THE UNITED STATES OF AMERICA

To
Julie and Pan

FOREWORD

THIS is a group of sketches about people who are doing things to-day; the writers and artists who are making our literature and designing the most beautiful of the illustrated books that each season, about Christmas time, tempt the book-lover beyond endurance. With the exception of Selma Lagerlöf, who, although she is still actively writing some of her most significant work, is so firmly ensconced in the Hall of Fame that she has become a classic, and "Elizabeth," who, no difference how many wise and witty books she may write, became a legend with the *German Garden*, these are people about whom the smoke and confusion of our vivid workaday world has not yet cleared away. They belong neither to the precocious youngsters nor to the established demigods. Theirs is the present, and they are so busy making it, so lustily experimenting with it, their work is so full of fascinating possibilities, that one cannot catch them in perspective or halt them for appraisal. Therefore, these sketches are in no sense critical. They are informal little stories, mostly biographical, about twenty-four contemporary artists and writers and work they are doing.

A. P. C.

CONTENTS

LIST OF ILLUSTRATIONS

"ELIZABETH"

JULIE BROWN

AUTHORS AND OTHERS

"ELIZABETH"

A Wise and Witty Legend

A WISE publisher once said that every so often in the cycle of literary fashions comes the appropriate moment for an anonymous novel. Perhaps so, but to us the lure of the unknown has no season. There is never a day when those bold or tender or wistful little lyrics marked "anon" in our anthologies do not stir a feeling of gentle curiosity about the unnamed writers whose moods are thus crystallized for our delight. And the anonymous authors of novels are even more interesting, for one likes to speculate about the environment, the circumstances of life, and the habits of mind that have produced the story. Almost always, if a book wins wide popularity, the name of the author becomes common knowledge, even though it is not announced in print. Such feats as that of Ray Stannard Baker, who lived for more than a score of years a double life as himself and David Grayson, the rustic philosopher of Hempfield; and that of "Elizabeth," who wrote a dozen widely read books under the cumbersome *nom de plume* "the author of *Elizabeth and Her German Garden*," before she was identified as the Countess Russell, are rare in contemporary history. Yet "Elizabeth" is so warmly personal and subjective a writer that her refusal to give interviews and talk about the details of her private life for publication does not really affect our knowledge of her. Such books as *Elizabeth and Her German Garden* are as distinctly autobiographical as *Mårbacka*, and much more vividly pictorial than many a serious *Life and Works*. So it happened that when, a few months ago, her friend Sir Philip Gibbs was permitted to write the first interview which "Elizabeth" has ever granted, he found very little to add.

Most of us made our acquaintance with "Elizabeth" when *Elizabeth and Her German Garden* was first published in 1898. It was written in the blithe spirit of the early twenties, when not even the arrival of the April, May, and June babies could entirely occupy her attention. Those first years as a German Countess, spent in maintaining the formal dignity and mediæval state of her position as the mistress of her husband's estate of sixty thousand acres, were a continual adventure to the gay-hearted, bright-haired young English girl, who delighted in spading the flowers when the gardener was not looking and lunching on salads under the lilac bushes when the "Man of Wrath" was away, instead of sitting alone in state in the lofty dining room.

"Elizabeth" was a schoolgirl in her teens when she met Count von Arnim. She was spending a holiday with her father in Italy, playing among the picture galleries and the pagan ruins, and going to tea in the dim old palaces of Roman high society. Von Arnim was twenty-five years older than she; very blond and tall and German, but, curiously enough, a liberal, although he belonged to one of the famous old Junker families to whom their nationalist caste was as sacred as their religion. He was the only son of the Ambassador Count Henry von Arnim, who was broken politically by the Iron Chancellor.

He married this flamelike young girl with her gold hair and romantic notions of love, and carried her away to an estate in East Prussia, where she spent most of the next twenty years.

Von Arnim was, as the Southern planters phrase it, "land poor." He was the master of great estates, a huge patriarchal system of tenants, crops, barns, cattle, a charming old château with numberless servants, nurses, governesses, which had to be maintained in mediæval state; and not much actual cash. The house stood in the middle of a vast Pomeranian plain, a rambling building of gray stone and many gables. The vaulted hall, with its worn brick floor, was once the chapel of a convent, but during the Thirty Years' War, Gustavus Adolphus passed through and turned the nuns out on to the plain to find some other shelter. There was one neighbour ten miles away

3

with whom the Von Arnims exchanged yearly calls. "Elizabeth" asked this pleasant Junker and his wife to dinner at Nassenheide in the winter, and they invited the Von Arnims to dinner in the summer. "Elizabeth" looked with something of awe at this energetic country lady who managed her troop of flaxen-haired children; superintended the feeding of the stock, the butter and sausage-making; drove around in her pony carriage to oversee the tenant farms; and boxed the careless dairymaid's ears. But the young mistress of Nassenheide, whose days were filled with the delights of her babies, her garden, and her books, could never quite see the necessity of cooking, sewing, and sausage-making, when the cooks and the maids did it all so much better and there was not half enough time in the world to be completely happy with the dandelions and the daisies.

When she and the April, May, and June babies were first transplanted to the estate in Pomerania, "Elizabeth" found a wilderness that would challenge the heart of any gardener. The paths were effaced by exuberant grass, periwinkles, and Solomon's Seal, and the neglected lawns were glowing with bird cherries, lilacs, and Virginia creeper. Discovering this abandoned garden was the beginning of her real life, she says. "It was my coming of age, as it were, and entering into my kingdom." That first summer was occupied with pansies and roses and dwarf mignonette; making beds about the sundials; comparing the virtues

4

of Duke of Teck, Cheshunt Scarlet, and Prefet de Limburg; and learning, as every gardener learns, by mistakes. But there were also pleasant hours of writing on the verandah, for "Elizabeth" did not retire behind locked doors to shut out interruption. One little picture of such a morning we remember in her diary:

"The three babies, more persistent than mosquitoes, are raging around me, and already several of the thirty fingers have been in the ink pot and the owners consoled when duty pointed to rebukes. But who can rebuke such penitent and drooping sunbonnets? I can see nothing but sunbonnets and pinafores and nimble black legs."

As the years slipped away, "Elizabeth" never took her household solemnly, never outgrew a secret amusement at the servants in their scarlet liveries; the formal dinners with her husband; the babies; and the silent tutors and governesses who, according to custom, did not speak until the Count or Countess spoke; the cooks and maids and gardeners who were horrified if she pruned a bush or touched a spade. During these years, the April, May, and June babies grew taller and the garden more beautiful. During these years the books by "Elizabeth" also grew in number and brought wide recognition for the witty and charming unknown, although she was scarcely aware of it, for fame found it hard to penetrate the fastnesses of Pomerania. Nine books belong to this period, the first two garden volumes: *Elizabeth and Her German Garden* and *The Solitary Summer;* and in succession, *April Baby's Book of Tunes, Adventures of Elizabeth in Rügen, The Princess Priscilla's Fortnight, Fräulein Schmidt and Mr. Anstruther, The Benefactress, The Caravaners,* and *The Pastor's Wife.* Of these the garden diary, although it was published nearly thirty years ago, still retains its lead in popularity and goes into new editions season after season.

The Solitary Summer is, in a sense, a continuation of *Elizabeth and Her German Garden.* Remembering her dream of a cottage at the edge of a little wood of silver birches by an amiable meandering stream, starred with yellow flags, a pathless place just big enough to hold herself and a baby, "Elizabeth" began to think how delightful a summer would be entirely by herself. "Two paradises 'twere in one, to live in Paradise alone" was a true song, she thought, but hardly the argument to quote to the "Man of Wrath." On May Day evening, in the garden full of stars and scents of sweet wallflowers and pansies, she asked him for a whole summer alone to idle and loaf with her soul. Although he could not understand her whim, the "Man of Wrath" was indulgent.

"Very well, my dear," he consented, "only don't grumble afterward if you find it dull. It is always best to allow a woman to do as she likes if you can, and it saves a good deal of bother. To have what she desires is generally an effective punishment."

This second garden book has the charm of the first, but one misses the babies, the "Man of Wrath" himself, and some of the gay, humorous touches that make "Elizabeth's" people, even the most casual of the governesses, amusingly human.

Adventures of Elizabeth in Rügen is the last book in which the young Grafin wrote of her own experiences in the first person. In this story of her trip around Rügen, Germany's big island in the Baltic Sea, "Elizabeth" indulges in her rollicking sense of the ridiculous, which was to reappear with a more satirical edge in such books as *The Caravaners* and *The Pastor's Wife*. To walk around the island was an alluring project, but the women of her acquaintance were appalled at the suggestion and could not be persuaded, not even by the argument that the exercise would be excellent for the German nation, especially those portions of it that were yet to come. So "Elizabeth" drove in a light victoria behind a pair of horses "esteemed at home for their meekness." Accompanied by August, the coachman; Gertrud, the maid; August's wet weather hat; the tea basket; innumerable bundles; and the inevitable shiny yellow wooden bandbox, "into which every decent German woman put her best hat," she spent a diverting holiday, getting lost on the road and floating with the beautiful jellyfish in the sandy coves along the way.

"Elizabeth's" next book was a venture in pure fiction, *The Princess Priscilla's Fortnight*, the tale

7

of her Grand Ducal Highness the Princess Priscilla of Lothen-Kunitz, a vivacious young lady with red-gold hair and a nose that was not quite straight. Having spent twenty-one years at the top of the social ladder, she decided to spend the next twenty-one at the bottom of it, and as the nicest place to live at the bottom was England, she ran away. Abetted by the Ducal Librarian, she spent a glorious holiday at Creeper Cottage, but ended by marrying the very prince from whom she had fled a fortnight earlier.

Two years later "Elizabeth" adventured in a new literary form, a comedy of manners in letters. *Fräulein Schmidt and Mr. Anstruther* records the progress of a romance between Fräulein Rose-Marie and her "Dear Roger." The letters are Rose-Marie's. At least, they started as letters, reams and reams of them, but after she decided that she would be a sister to him, the correspondence languished. Wounded that he did not prove a faithful lover, indeed not even a faithful friend after she told him about her helpful sisterly attitude, she made her communications brief, finally limiting her last five letters to one sentence each, in this order:

"It would be useless."
"I would not see you."
"I do not love you."
"I will never marry you."
"I shall not write again."

8

In this history of a blighted romance, "Elizabeth" indulges in gentle irony, but in *The Caravaners*, her gift for satire is for the first time fully employed. One cannot remember a more devastating picture of a Prussian army officer than this self-drawn portrait of the lazy, pompous, miserly Baron von Ottringel, yet withal so stupid and childlike that he wins the reader's grudging sympathy. But even in her most biting moods, "Elizabeth's" merriment cannot be suppressed. There is something so irresistibly funny about Edelgard's rebellion, abetted by the attractive Frau von Eckthum, with the scandalously small feet and the dark eyelashes; not to mention Jellaby, the unspeakable socialist; and Browne, who turned out to be not plain Browne at all, but Lord Sigismund Brown, the youngest son of The Duke of Hereford and the nephew of the Princess of Grossburg-Niederhausen.

It has been said sometimes that perhaps the Baron von Ottringel was a portrait of the Count von Arnim, but we have "Elizabeth's" word for it that he was not. Her husband appeared in none of her works except the two garden books, and it is evident that she had a very deep affection and admiration for the "Man of Wrath."

In 1910, "Elizabeth's" pleasant, isolated life in Pomerania came to an end. The husband, who loved her devotedly, died, and without him she began to feel the differences of opinion and the racial hostilities that separated her from his

countrymen and his kin. There is another book,
however, that belongs to this German period, one
of the most wistful and potentially tragic stories
that she has done, yet at the same time one of her
most amusing both in character drawing and
situations: *The Pastor's Wife*. Ingeborg, the plain
young daughter of the Bishop of Redchester, who
in one mad moment of escape from the Bishop's
gaiter buttons, the Bishop's speeches, his correspondence, and his tea parties, got carried away
by a scientific German pastor, who forgot his
fertilizers long enough to fall in love with her, is
just such a direct, romantic, ignorant young
creature as "Elizabeth" was herself when she
set off for Prussia years ago. Her eagerness to
adjust her joyous, pliable little self to the stiff and
formal customs of her Prussian neighbours, her
cheerful abandonment to bearing little Prussians,
her final rebellion and readjustment to a bewil-
dering solitude, shut out from her husband's
thoughts, is a story of such poignancy that the
diverting episode of Edward Ingram, the great
artist, who wanted to capture her soul, is just so
much whipped cream on a rich pastry.

The Pastor's Wife is the last of "Elizabeth's"
books that has a German setting, and its appearance marked the end of her own life in Germany.
It had been Count von Arnim's wish that his
children be educated in England, so their mother
joined them there and sent her son to Eton. When
the war broke out, the youngest daughter, the

June baby, was in Germany and was unable to get away. She married a Bavarian and remained German in sympathies, but it happens that "Elizabeth" and her son-in-law like each other, so there is no discord in the family. Early in the war, "Elizabeth" regained her English citizenship through her marriage to Earl Russell. After three years, there was a separation, and now "Elizabeth" has returned to her writing and her friends and her children. During these later years, her reputation as a writer has steadily increased, and with it her fame as one of the wittiest and most popular of London's hostesses. Her April and May babies, who were not entirely happy in England during the war, came to the United States and have since married Americans. Their adventures are the basis, very much altered as to fact, of that amazing odyssey, *Christopher and Columbus*. In the story "Elizabeth" names the April and May babies Anna-Rose and Anna-Felicitas, and makes them seventeen-year-old twins; Anna-Rose the elder by twenty minutes. Although they were very German outside with their fair hair and blue eyes, they were very English inside. But this was something which a British uncle, who did not like orphaned alien nieces, could never understand, so he shipped them to some vaguely remembered friends in America with a letter of introduction and five hundred pounds. On the boat, as they were looking disconsolately at a vast deal of dreadfully wet sea and pretending to be thoroughly happy, they named themselves Christopher and Columbus, setting sail to discover America. Instead, it was Mr. Twist who discovered them. Mr. Twist was an American engineer with ample means and, being a "disciplined son and brother," he thought much in his cabin—one with a private bathroom—about those two defenseless children who were being set adrift in a strange and none too hospitable land. So it happened that Mr. Twist appointed himself their guardian, took them to California, invested in a tea room which Anna-Rose and Anna-Felicitas furnished with sea-blue cushions and flower pots and a canary, and found himself and the twins involved in such ludicrous and compromising situations that there was nothing else to do but marry one of them.

With her two daughters and her son married in America, and her June baby married in Germany, "Elizabeth" found more time to devote to her writing than she had ever known. Consequently, the past few years have been her most productive ones. After the separation from Lord Russell, she spent long summers in Switzerland at her "Chalet Soleil," perched high on a green shoulder of the Alps. Here much of the next book, *Vera*, was written, the book in which "Elizabeth" reaches the heights of her power as a satirist. To begin with, Vera, the heroine, if one may call her such, is dead when the story opens, but her spirit so pervades the tale that in the end her successor,

Lucy, the gentle, simple, pretty young second wife of Wemyss, begins to wonder if perhaps Vera's fall from the second-story window was not suicide after all. And Wemyss himself is a character etched in such sharp clear lines that he immediately becomes one of the unforgettable fiction people. The meanest man in fiction, the critics called him, and it would be difficult to think of a competitor for the title. *Vera* was the book which led Mrs. Meynell to call "Elizabeth" one "of the three finest wits of our day," and there is ample justification for her choice. "Elizabeth's" metaphors have an aptness and a whimsical quality that give a distinct fillip to her style. Lucy's Everard, for instance, was so comfortable to lean on mentally. "Bodily, on the few occasions on which her aunt was out of the room, he was comfortable, too; he reminded her of the very nicest of sofas—expensive ones, all cushions. But mentally he was more than comfortable, he was positively luxurious. Such perfect rest listening to him talk." Miss Entwhistle, the intrepid little aunt, who dared to tell Everard that Lucy had not the staying powers of Vera, before she was turned out into the night without a hat, is one of the most likable and human women that "Elizabeth" has done. Although *Vera* is written in a sardonic mood, there are many lighter humorous touches, reminiscent of the earlier *Christopher and Columbus* and *The Pastor's Wife*.

After expressing her devastating opinion of the

13

genus homo, "Elizabeth" turned to happier things,
to wisteria and sunshine and the miracle that
scenic loveliness works on tired humans. Her next
book, *The Enchánted April,* is rivalled by none of
her others except perhaps *Elizabeth and Her
German Garden.* It contains also some of the most
sparkling examples of her wit. Of Frederick, Mrs.
Arbuthnot's errant husband, she gives fleeting
pictures, sketches with a certain tolerant delight.
He "had been the kind of husband whose wife
betakes herself early to the feet of God. From him
to them had been a short, though painful, step.
From her passionately loved bridegroom, from her
worshipped young husband, he had become second
only to God on her list of duties and forbear-
ances." And again, "Her very nest egg was the
fruit, posthumously ripened, of ancient sin."
The way Frederick made his living was one of the
standing distresses of her life. He wrote immensely
popular memoirs, regularly every year, of the
mistresses of Kings.

"There were in history numerous Kings who
had mistresses, and there were still more numerous
mistresses who had had Kings, so that he had been
able to publish a book of memoirs during each
year of his married life, and even so there were
great further piles of these ladies waiting to be
dealt with. The more the memoired lady had
forgotten herself, the more his book about her
was read and the more free-handed he was to his

wife. The parish flourished because, to take a handful at random, of the ill behaviour of the ladies Du Barry, Montespan, Pompadour, Ninon de l'Enclos and even of the learned Maintenon. The poor were the filter through which the money was passed, to come out, Mrs. Arbuthnot hopes, purified. Their very boots were stout with sins."

In this tale of the four runaway ladies in the Italian castle, "Elizabeth" breaks occasionally into hilarity that borders on farce. The bathroom scene, in which the eccentric Italian water heater explodes and ejects the dignified solicitor Mellerish Wilkins, clad in a bath towel, into the presence of the lovely Lady Caroline Dexter, none other than the daughter of the Droitwiches, needs very little dramatization to transform it into an excellent vaudeville sketch. But, above all, the book breathes the beauty of gardens and sea and sky and the happiness that one may find in shaking himself free of mundane affairs and very simply enjoying the blessings of being alive. It is the old "Elizabeth" who danced for joy among the blue hepaticas and celandines of that far-away Pomeranian garden, but an "Elizabeth" with a freer spirit. Then, being very young, she danced behind a bush, mindful of her "years and children and having due regard for the decencies." In *The Enchanted April* she dances again for joy, but, being older and wiser, more conscious of the preciousness and rarity of joy, she dances gloriously in the centre of the lawn.

Like all of "Elizabeth's" books, *The Enchanted April* is the picture of a place which she knows well. The original of the castle of the wisteria and the lilacs is the Castello of Portofino, a gracious old group of towers, dating from the Crusades. It is on the Gulf of Rapallo and looks down over the little village of Portofino, in whose church rest the relics of St. George of the dragon fame.

From the Puck-like delights of *The Enchanted April*, "Elizabeth" touches in her next book, *Love*, a theme that is essentially tragic: the love of a young man and an older woman. Carried away by the impetuosity of his wooing, Catherine married Christopher, in spite of the fact that she had a married daughter who was almost as old as he. "Elizabeth's" picture of this charming, sensible, middle-aged woman, who from loving fell in love, is one of the most poignant character studies that she has done. Catherine's grotesque efforts to stay young for him, and her final decision that she could no longer live a deception when the shock of her daughter's death revealed suddenly the marks of years, are among the unspoken tragedies that are too painful to read with enjoyment. Nor is Christopher's plight any the more happy, for he loved her with a genuine devotion.

"Good God, Catherine," he pleads, "do you think a man wants his wife to scrub herself with yellow soap as if she were the kitchen table, and then come all shiny to him and say, 'See, I am the Truth'? And she isn't the Truth. She's no more the truth shiny than powdered. She's only appearance anyway. She's only a symbol—the symbol of the spirit in her which is what one is loving the whole time."

But the fact remains between them, and "Elizabeth" offers no solution. She leaves them trying to laugh, "but it was a shaky, uncertain laughter, for they were both afraid."

As a comic relief, "Elizabeth" is on a glorious holiday in her hilarious *Introduction to Sally*, a tale in which she laughs at love and beauty and misplaced "h's," culture and elderly suitors, and all the other amusing ingredients of this decorous world. The innocent cause of her amusement is Sally Pinner, whose beauty is so bright that the customers of her father's little shop never notice her lapses in grammar. On her serene and devastating way, Sally meets and subdues a garage mechanic with a bucket of Irish stew, a marquis with an untouched glacial heart, a deaf old duke whose eyesight is unimpaired, not to mention a prospective father-in-law and all the casual passers-by who chanced to see her glory. It is an odyssey of amusing episodes done in the countess's most impish humour.

Sally brings "Elizabeth's" literary history to date, fifteen books in almost as many moods, and, it is rumoured by those who know her, at least two others published entirely anonymously. What she will do next, one cannot prophesy, for she is still in her prime. One's only safe conjecture is that her next book will be unlike her last. Although she is a grandmother, "Elizabeth" looks and is surprisingly young. She has retained the delicate colouring and flowery grace of a Dresden china figure, but with all her gracious femininity, there is a boldness and keen mental alertness, both in her writings and her conversation, that justify Alice Meynell's choosing her as one of the three great wits among our contemporaries.

CHARLES B. FALLS

Charles B. Falls

CHARLES B. FALLS

Book-maker to a Very Young Lady

MISTRESS BEDELIA JANE FALLS—aged five—is a young lady of the moment in the art world. Two of the most decorative books of the past few seasons were designed and illustrated for her by one of New York's most distinguished poster-artists, all that the winsome little girl might learn her letters and her nursery rhymes from books of her very own. Furthermore, it is rumoured in literary circles that the royalties of these sprightly books are bequeathed in perpetuity to the lady of their inspiration. These volumes are the beautiful animal *A B C Book*, illustrated with twenty-six woodcuts, and a gayly decorated special edition of *Mother Goose*, both of which Doubleday, Page & Company consider among the most beautiful volumes, from the point of view of illustrations and book making, that have come from their presses in the past few years. And the explanation of Bedelia Jane's early preoccupation with the arts is that she is the only daughter of Charles B. Falls, whose posters have won him such high rank among his fellow artists that he is considered by many—notably the late Joseph Pennell

19

—the best colour printer in America. In his studio high up in an office building overlooking Madison Square, Mr. Falls cut the animals for the A B C Book in odd moments, sandwiched in between his classes at the Art Students' League, the school for disabled soldiers, and commissions that pressed for completion. The studio has none of the attributes that dilettantes have connected with the term. It is a real workshop. Under the window is a large desk with a drawing board, pens, pencils, brushes, ink bottles, paints, stray scraps of paper, bits of designs, and a miscellany of battered manila envelopes scattered over its top. In the opposite corner is a table completely banked in with sketches, large, small, and middle-sized, on wood, cardboard, and paper; more manila envelopes; and a few stray books. Between them is a large stuffed armchair, broken down and supremely comfortable. Over the back of a chair is a black coat splashed with twice as many colours as there are in the rainbow.

Mr. Falls himself is a small, plump man with quick eyes and hands, a gentle manner and a quiet voice. He has won his success in New York, but his career actually began a good many years ago in an architect's office in Chicago. The boy had drifted into architecture by chance, for he had no interest in the arts. His real ambition was to be a lawyer, because he had the youthful delusion that all lawyers are very clever men. The next stepping stone was the art staff of the Chicago *Tribune*, but he did not stay there long, for, when the management refused to raise his salary from twelve to fifteen dollars a week, he recklessly challenged fate by throwing up his job and coming to New York. Then followed years of the sort of struggle that makes good material for sentimental novels but has its drawback in real life, according to Mr. Falls—nights in the park, months of hand-to-mouth existence in cheap boarding houses, day upon day of ceaseless work with the encouragement of an occasional sale, until finally fate got tired of the long-drawn-out duel and gave him the victory.

A real artist's first requisite is an unquenchable love of his work, believes Mr. Falls. Years ago, when he first determined upon his career, it was not a lucrative profession, and the only incentive was the actual joy one got from his work. But within the past ten years conditions have changed. Commercial art has become a highly paid business and has attracted many clever young men whose only concern is making money. "Indeed," says Mr. Falls, "many of the younger generation look upon art, not as a radiant and beautiful maiden to be wooed, but as an old woman with a lot of money."

Although Mr. Falls disclaims connection with the younger generation, it will be many years before he belongs to the older generation. In fact, as long as his work has the buoyant vitality of Bedelia Jane's *A B C Book*, he can't convincingly claim a sober middle age.

21

ELLEN GLASGOW

ELLEN GLASGOW

Her Jeremy Looks at Life

JEREMY, as befits a dog of quality, looks at life with superior, and not too evident, curiosity from the high stone steps of Miss Ellen Glasgow's doorway. It is a dignified, aged, gray Colonial brick house with an old-fashioned garden behind it. To be sure, the city has crowded up around it and Richmond's best families have long since moved away, but Jeremy rather approves of his mistress's affection for the old mansion and her pleasure in keeping it in the manner of its former spacious days. He likes the fine old mahogany and the high ceilings of the rooms that are rooms, each with its own real fireplace that will burn, and the little garden with its crooked path. "So English," he comments to his ward, a little white puffball of a poodle. For Jeremy, of course, is English, very English indeed. He was given to Miss Glasgow by Hugh Walpole, who calls this house on Main Street his American home. Being a Britisher and accustomed to move in the best literary circles, Jeremy was a bit stand-offish at first with the Richmond literati. It is even said that he deliberately sniffed at the first lump of sugar offered him

23

by James Branch Cabell. However, they are now excellent friends, for Jeremy was quick to recognize Cabell's cosmopolitanism. Mary Johnston he also accepted unconditionally, for she knows so much about the Elizabethans and the Georges, and has a remarkable understanding of an Englishman's traditions. But when such breezy and forthright Westerners as William Allen White drop in for a visit, he is stirred with a disturbing dream of going West to seek his fortune on the wind-swept ranges that he hears are somewhere beyond the Kansas wheat belt. Yet one cannot desert one's responsibilities, and poodles are addicted to a life of ease.

Though he lives in the effete East in one of the loveliest and laziest cities in America, Jeremy is by no means a dog of leisure. He has his work to do and believes in doing it faithfully and thoroughly. He is Miss Glasgow's collaborator. In the morning, when she starts upstairs to the big front study with its rows upon rows of autographed volumes, Jeremy is always ready, too. She locks the door to shut out interruption, and the two of them settle to work on the novel in hand. Miss Glasgow has written many books, some of them before Jeremy came, but he is secretly a bit jealous of them and confident in his doggish heart that they aren't quite so good as those written with his assistance. It is a pleasant room, this study, lined with bookshelves, but there is a crisp briskness about it that is characteristic of its owner when she is writing or talking about books and the making of them. For, although she is intensely feminine, with a slim, svelte feminity that delights in wearing tones of brown to set off her curling, red-bronze hair, Jeremy senses that his mistress has a masculine mind, that she is a keen, rational, unemotional realist who refuses to see life other than as it is, but misses none of the colour and drama of it because she is not carried away by a sentiment or an illusion.

In this room the child Ellen began and completed her schooling. The delicate little girl was given no formal education, so she grew up in a happy companionship with books. Here, before her eighteenth birthday, she wrote *The Descendant* which so interested Walter Hines Page that he urged her to rewrite parts of it, and published it anonymously. It was not until the appearance of the third book, *The Voice of the People*, that her name appeared as the author. Although she was as sheltered and far removed from unpleasant actualities as the heroine of her favourite novel *Virginia*, there was iron in Ellen Glasgow's veins. She appreciates the glamour and charm of the romantic tradition; she likes to visualize the generals and statesmen and belles of an earlier age who danced the Sir Roger de Coverley and sipped punch in the double parlours. She delights in her setting of fine old mahogany, Colonial silver, and demure, stone-flagged gardens that one generation cannot grow. But she sees also this

25

tradition's inadequacies and absurdities. In her first story, *The Descendant*, she developed a theme which was to characterize much of her work, the fusing of the old aristocracy with the more virile strain of the common people. The descendant was an "intellectual hybrid," the son of a brilliant, well-born father and a low mother. *The Voice of the People* is the study of an overseer who has bought his master's estate. Through *The Battle-Ground*, *Life and Gabriella*, *The Romance of a Plain Man*, *One Man in His Time*, and, more recently, *Barren Ground*, has run the common thread of interest, the struggle of the old South against the new, the last pathetic and gently ridiculous stand of the romantic age against the vigorous stirring of the new elements that are building a powerful modern structure on the wreckage of an outworn ideal. In *The Romantic Comedians* she has set out like a modern Cervantes to strike a death blow to this tradition with the rapier of her wit.

But although she is essentially a realist, Miss Glasgow's realism is not of the sordid kind. Her irony is tempered by a sense of humour and a delightful impartiality toward all of her characters, and she is no crusader. Good humour, a vigorous wit, and facility of expression make her as good a conversationalist as she is a writer. There is a vitality about her, a sparkle that inevitably makes her the most vivid personality in any gathering.

So it is a pleasant world that Jeremy surveys

from his doorstep, a little bit of the charm and glamour of the Old Dominion carried over into an alien age, and to this friendly little dog with the aristocratic nose, it is more real than all those barren fields of broomsedge about which his mistress writes.

GORDON GRANT

Gordon Grant

GORDON GRANT

Painter of Clipper Ships

IN SAN FRANCISCO, in the days when the
Panama Canal was a dream and rounding the
Horn part of the day's work in the life of many
a blue-water sailor, Gordon Grant got his first
view of the tall ships that were to make him
famous. Sometimes there were as many as fifty
or sixty fine sailing ships in the harbour at once,
barkentines and three and four masters that ran
like hounds before the wind. The boy's father had
many friends among the captains of these vessels
and through them he knew well many of the famous ships that have passed into memory.

When he was twelve years old, Gordon's Scots
parents sent him home to Scotland to school. Com-
mitted to the care of the skipper of the smart
Glasgow ship, *City of Madras*, he spent four
months on the way. It was a fascinating school of
sea lore to the eager youngster, who managed to
find unholy entertainment in the fo'c'sle in spite of
the captain's "don'ts." The master was a pious
disciplinarian, who forbade the boy's going aloft,
but at the end of the voyage there was no more

29

hardened little salt afloat, or one with a more precocious knowledge of sea jargon and profanity picked up from the crew. The impressionable boy with the passion for drawing had fallen in love with the sea and everything afloat.

For the next six years Grant lived in a seaport town in Fifeshire, when the North Sea craft from the Baltic crowded the picturesque harbour. Every spare moment the boy spent at the docks where they were loading and discharging, loafing with the sailors and asking a thousand questions.

At eighteen, Grant was on his way to Glasgow to be articled to one of the great shipbuilding firms on the Clyde, with the intention of becoming a marine architect, but Fate stepped in, and he found himself not in Glasgow but in London studying art.

Two years later, Grant was back in San Francisco with a position on the staff of the *Examiner*. But New York, the Mecca of artists, was his ultimate destination, and within a year he was working in the art department of the Sunday *World*. From then on, his work as an illustrator won rapid recognition. In 1899, he was sent to South Africa for *Harper's Weekly* as special artist at the front during the Boer War, and later was for nine years on the staff of *Puck*. But always there was a distinct leaning toward ships and the sea. During the past years he has practically abandoned everything else to perpetuate in his paintings the memory of the clipper ships which made America for a brief era the queen of the seas. And whenever he feels that his seamanship is getting threadbare he gets into first-hand touch with the sea. Last spring he shipped aboard a square-rigged ship out of San Francisco, one of the few old-timers left.

Gordon Grant's technical knowledge of sailing ships and their intricacies is the admiration of many an old salt who knows all there is to know about sails and rig, and he has incorporated this knowledge in the beautiful book of maritime lore, *The Book of Old Ships*, by Henry Culver, the secretary of the Ship Model Society, for which Grant drew the vivid end papers and the numberless line drawings of types and details of ships, tracing their complete history under sail. Mr. Grant is also one of the founders of the Ship Model Society.

For some years, the Maine coast has been both Grant's playground and his workshop. When he is not doing marine canvases, he is finding amusement at his carpenter's bench and in doing costumes and scenery for amateur dramatics. He is a robust and jolly spirit. Jazz, noisy people, and the modernist art movement, which he calls the yowl of the incompetent who fancies he can get into the limelight by short cuts, are his only pronounced aversions, though Broadway and Forty-second Street and bobbed hair are also catalogued by him as things to be avoided. The fascination of the sea is as strong upon him now as it was upon the fourteen-year-old boy who sailed years ago on the crack Glasgow square-rigger, and his greatest pleasure is to record in his canvases the glamorous story of the age of sail.

ELIZABETH MacKINSTRY

Elizabeth MacKinstry

ELIZABETH MACKINSTRY

An Intimate Friend of the Fairies

AMONG us the art of fine book-making is suffering a revival. With Bruce Rogers designing formats, Gowdy cutting new types, and many a young printer and advertising man collecting *The Fleuron* and the best examples of contemporary German, French, and Viennese book-making, the general appearance of all books, even the novels that flood the spring book counters in casual thousands, is vastly more pleasing to the eye. And the artist has come into his own. The sickly oil or wash illustrations of heroines, on horrible glazed paper, looking soulfully at the heroes in from four to six different attitudes, tipped into the books at appropriate intervals, are no longer demanded of them. The very word, "illustration," has suffered an eclipse. No longer does the artist slavishly draw some actual moment described in the text, after the manner of the photographer who tells all too well the tragedy of the young man who didn't devote fifteen minutes a day to a self-improvement course. His work is now an integral part of the book, indivisible from the text as the dance from music. He does not repeat

33

what the author has said already, but embellishes, expresses in his own medium the spirit of the text, setting the key for the author's mood, unifying and intensifying the impression that the author strives to create, in line and colour which have a definite decorative value of their own.

Among the younger artists who have been busy during the past few years in decorating some of the most beautiful books that have found their way to the shops, Elizabeth MacKinstry has perhaps contributed more volumes than any other to the delight of fine-book lovers. Although she turned from sculpture to book decoration only three years ago, she has done within that time several elfin children's books of exquisite imaginative humour and three volumes of genuine distinction. Her own book of poems, *Puck in Pasture*, which established her both as poet and artist, her sketches for Percy MacKaye's *Tall Tales*, and the drawings for the new edition of *Tales of Laughter* place her among the foremost of contemporary illustrators.

Two of the most striking characteristics of her work, the roundness of line, which gives her figures a sculptured effect, and the rhythm of her composition, Miss MacKinstry attributes to her early devotion to two other arts, sculpture and music. For she is one of those upon whom the gods shower gifts. In her 'teens the child was one of Ysaye's favourite pupils, with a continental reputation as a violinist, and very little later, when the violin had to be put away, she studied modelling under

the aged Rodin and worked in wood for Ralph
Adams Cram.

From the moment that the father, discouraged
by his tiny daughter's pale, anæmic features,
instructed that she be stripped of her spotless
white dresses and left to play on the terrace clothed
in turkey red to attract the sun, baby Elizabeth's
eyes were observant of colour and form. The
clouds and trees, the steeps and pleasant valleys
glowing in the sunshine of southern France, where
the family spent the winters, left many a vivid
picture in her memory. And the world of make-
believe, which is to many children more true
than the reality, was peopled with all the fairies
and hobgoblins of French folklore. Lisa, the cook,
in a black dress and black silk apron with a gay
kerchief twisted about her black braids, was the
little girl's dearest companion next to the big
collie dog which had been her nurse since she had
made her first essays to crawl. Lisa knew all the
legends and fairy tales of France.

At seven, Elizabeth was such a promising violinist that she went to Paris to study. Then began
years of gruelling work, for little violin prodigies
practise about seven hours a day. There was no
school, but a governess wedged in what study
there was between practice periods and the three
hours devoted to walking every day. Those hours
were gloriously free. In the winter it rained about
four days out of seven, and then the child played
in the Louvre and the Luxemburg until both of

35

the galleries became as dear and familiar to her as one's grandmother's attic. And then there were the summer vacations. One spent in Scotland, Miss MacKinstry looks back upon as the happiest holiday of her life. The nine-year-old child and her mother visited all the places of the old ballads. Brig o' Doon, Banks of Yarrow, the tomb of the grand old wizard, Michael Scott. The little tousled-haired pilgrim wore a plaid and proudly carried a copy of Sir Walter Scott's poems. In Edinburgh she saw a panorama play of *The Lady of the Lake*. The hero and the heroine interested her not at all, but she was so captivated by the villain, Roderick Dhu, and wept so stormily at his death, that she had to be taken out and shaken before she could see the rest of it. There were other summers in Ireland, at Barbizon, playing in the forest, and trips to Thuringia to the forest of Tannhäuser. In the old castle of Wartburg she heard a hoen playing, and that, she is certain, made her a romantic for life. Certain it is that the child had collected the folk and fairy lore of half the countries in Europe.

At fifteen, Elizabeth went to Brussels to study with Ysaye. Learning that he required some very difficult scales, she studied them with a pupil of his for three weeks. And it was fortunate that she did, for when Ysaye gave the girl a trial, things did not go well. Wedged in between a temporary wood stove and the piano in his enormous music room, timid and half frightened by the Master,

who loomed above her like a Titan, and discon-
certed by the accompaniment which he played
himself and vilely (Beethoven's Romance in F),
the child was conscious that she was making a
miserable failure.

"I see nothing in her," said Ysaye. "It is a cold
and timid little tone and talent."

"Could we try the scales, Master?" asked the
pupil who went along.

The scales were tried and, considering that
Elizabeth had practised them eight hours a day,
they went well.

"Prodigious industry," said Ysaye, and decided
that she should be his pupil.

But the first triumph came later. While Elizabeth was waiting at Ysaye's house for the first
lesson, as always with Ysaye one had to wait, she
played the Romance in F for herself; no talent,
no good, a very mournful, woebegone little fiddler.
In came Ysaye with his violin and said, "Go on."
He played the accompaniment this time on his
own instrument, and it was like an orchestra of the
gods. At the end he kissed her hand and said, "My
child, you have the temperament of an artist, but
do you eat enough beefsteak? You must eat twice,
once for yourself and once for the violin. The
temperament of the artist is much for a man, too
much for a woman."

That year only two passed for entry into the
conservatory, and Elizabeth MacKinstry was one
of them. It was a winter of vivid memories. There

was work, seven hours of it, at high tension, exulta-
tion when she won the Master's praise and black
despair when a lesson did not go so well. There
were dreams of the concert career that was to start
in Paris. But best of all were the violet dusks of
late afternoon when the girl walked home from the
conservatory with her violin under her arm.

During the next winter in Paris, Miss MacKinstry made her first formal acquaintance with art.
Hogarth's drawings had been favourites since she
was old enough to sprawl on the floor and demand
a picture book. And Sundays, her own days, were
always spent drawing. With the French idea that,
if you do a thing at all, you must do it well, her
mother decided that she might have art lessons; so,
after grave consultations with her music master, the
girl was allowed to spend some time at art school.

For several months she worked in Rodin's
studio. The old master was taking no new pupils,
but he did need a studio boy; so she carried about
the plaster and clay for the privilege of working
with him. The girl was so impressed with the
famous pupils who studied with the old giant that
she kept herself out of the way as much as possible,
modelling, in miniature, elfs and drolls and tiny
humorous figures. Although she tried to keep
them out of sight, they pleased Rodin immensely.
Whenever he had guests, he dragged her from her
corner by the ear and exhibited the exquisitely
modelled little grotesqueries. Rodin was so tall
that Elizabeth could stand under his arm, and it

amused him to walk past her and to pretend to be looking for her. The studio was often the scene of great discussions about art and literature and life in general, for Rodin's tremendous vitality made him one of the most vivid conversationalists that the girl had ever known.

After one brief season of concerts in England and France, concerts which gave promise of a brilliant career, there was an illness which meant the end of music for Elizabeth MacKinstry. At the same time, the little income, which had been dwindling through unwise investments, vanished altogether. There was a living to be made for two. Slowly she won back a grasp on life, in an old farmhouse near Buffalo. "Lost Orchards" she called it. A white winter followed, and the snow drifted into the room, for her windows and doors had been taken out; but the three Duncard sisters, who kept the house, brought books from the library when they carried their produce to town. In the barn, which she had fitted up as a studio, she relearned modelling and set out to earn her living by a new art.

A cousin who was a civil engineer gave Elizabeth some drafting to do, and she illustrated Hall Caine's *The Manxman* for a Buffalo paper. Looking back, she has a suspicion that the drawings were worthy of the publication, but she was immensely serious about them then.

It was at "Lost Orchards" that the first book of poems was written, *Helen's Mirror*, which so interested Alice Meynell that it was accepted for publication in a series of delightfully printed miniature books of single poems or small collections by distinguished English poets. *Helen's Mirror* was well received by the English press, and several of the lyrics were widely quoted. *Dream Children*, suggested by the sentence of Charles Lamb, "We are not the children of Alice, nor of thee, nor are we children at all . . . we are only that which might have been," is typical of the limpid clarity and Greek rhythm of them all.

Lullaby

"Light is rising o'er the daisies,
  Larks are singing in the corn,
  Little lambs are frisking, bleating
  T'ward the waiting pastures fleeting,
Lullaby, sweet babe unborn.

"Other mothers hush their nestlings
  In the sunset, I at morn;
  All the silver night I hold thee,
  Only then, in dreams enfold thee,
Lullaby, sweet babe unborn.

"Lullaby, sweet babe that lacks me.
  Lullaby, my heart is torn!
  In what clear and airy meadow
  Lurk'st thou, far beyond our shadow?
Lullaby, sweet babe unborn.

ELIZABETH MACKINSTRY

"In what verdant pasture playest?
  Little babe thou art forsworn,
  For thou dost disdain the portal,
  Little rosy child immortal,
Lullaby, sweet babe unborn."

Love at Night is in the same cool, fragrant mood:

"If all the gifts of the Seven Worlds
  Were within my keep,
I should give you but one to-night
That of the dark without any light
  And perfect sleep.

"All day long has the green world burned
  With a lambent fire,
And life laughed, spreading her tangled hair
To water and wind, in the dancing snare,
  Of which you tire.

"Now laughter and light should be put away
  And day should cease,
And Love also, like the sunset rose,
Should hush itself to a gray repose,
  A wordless peace.

"If all the gifts of the Seven Worlds
  Were within my keep,
I should give you but one—to-night,
That of the dark, without any light,
  And perfect sleep."

41

In a gustier and more robust spirit is *The Grave:*

> "Say life is thus and so, a feast
>   With honeyed fruit and wine outspread,
> A wind blows through the vaulted roof,
>   And sweeps us all into our bed.
>
> "And if it snuffs out drunken louts
>   Or wakens great bewildered gods—
> Ho, brother! tears are in your wine—
>   What matter? For to whom the odds?"

Miss MacKinstry saw the first copy of *Helen's Mirror* a year later in Capri. It had been proof-read by a Presbyterian minister who had made many emendations, but in spite of its errors the little volume was a thing of joy to the young author who had not yet reached her twentieth year.

It was at Capri that Miss MacKinstry met the late William Heinemann. The English publisher, with his flair for discovering talent, recognized in her an artist whose work could be well utilized in making beautiful books, so he offered her a book to illustrate, anything she wanted to select. Perhaps it was the very magnitude of the choice that bewildered the girl, for she could never quite decide what she wanted most to choose, so the book remained undone.

There were too many necessary things pressing for attention. First of all, she had to find regular employment, and this must be supplemented by every kind of work that one could discover. Her first opportunity was with a firm of tombstone makers. Carving little angels and doves with olive branches, scrolls, open Bibles, and half-draped urns was not, she realized, the form of art to which she had aspired, but the owner of the firm was a kindly old gentleman. In an age of automobiles he drove a sleek, unflurried horse to a high-wheeled trap, and there was something in his bland disregard of the rush of modern life that encouraged her. Then, too, there was a great need of improving tombstone design, so she set to work with zest.

Often stray commissions came to help meet the needs of the family. One which was particularly opportune, but which retains for her to this day the horror of a Poe tale, was a commission to make a death mask of an old gentleman who lay in a country house about an hour from town. Miss MacKinstry had never made a death mask; in fact, she knew nothing about making them, and the funeral was to be held on the following day. There was time to rush to the library, so the girl took an afternoon train with the information in a volume under her arm. The family had returned to town, and there was no one in the house except a superstitious housekeeper who refused to go near the room of the dead. With no assistance she worked through the night, a gusty winter one that rattled the shutters on the old house and shook

the window panes. The old gentleman's beard she
wrapped carefully to keep the plaster from sticking
to it, but for several sickening moments when she
pulled off the mask, she feared that there would
be no whiskers left.

The next few years were so full of a number of
things that Elizabeth MacKinstry had no time
for regretting the violin. She taught at the Al-
bright Art Gallery in Buffalo, and so many other
schools at the same time that it was hard to keep
count of them. Backed by European training
and utter serenity, she undertook to teach sculpture, life, design, anything. At first, if the classes
had to make an armature, she read up the process
in the library and tried it out with her pupils.
And it is surprising how often she succeeded.

No one but an artist would understand the richness of those hard years. They were a period of
self-training that was to be invaluable. She studied
sculpture as she taught it, she spent hours daily
drawing what she wanted to draw. She studied
illumination and was surprised to find how many
good illuminated manuscripts were to be found
in her own city available for use. From there she
learned to use clear flat colours with the brilliant
effect that the mediæval monks attained in their
intricately decorated initial letters. From a
wood-carver she learned to carve on wood. Her
little bronzes began to win recognition in the New
York galleries and were selected to make part of
an exhibition of the work of contemporary sculp-

tors that was sent throughout the country. In the summer there were trips abroad or time for her own work in the apple-orchard studio. To be sure, one required, as Ysaye said, "prodigious energy," but this she had.

To these years in "the provinces" Elizabeth MacKinstry attributes the measure of success that has later come to her. While it is true that there is no market for art except in the large cities, there are the libraries, the opportunity to find one's self before one plunges into commercial bondage, and a leisurely manner of living that leaves one's energies for his own work. "The provinces and an obscure job," that is her gospel to young artists. And she quotes in defense of her theory Rodin, who worked obscurely in Brussels as a sculptor's assistant and repairer of Gothic ornament for twenty years.

Nevertheless, when the mother died, and she dared risk real poverty if need be, Elizabeth MacKinstry forfeited the good "prospects" which lay before her in the art school and the museum, and came to New York. There she became associated with Ralph Adams Cram and spent several years working chiefly in wood on Gothic ornaments and ecclesiastical sculpture. This was a vivid period, for no one could come under the influence of such an artist as Mr. Cram without taking great strides both mentally and in craftsmanship.

Mr. Cram, thinks Elizabeth MacKinstry, is one

of those rare spirits who belong to another age and who manage to live in it and recreate it out of an alien civilization by the sheer power of their personality. She sees him as a great Twelfth Century artist, working, thinking, and creating in the Gothic style as naturally and inevitably as the architects of Notre Dame. But try however hard she might, Miss MacKinstry could never completely identify herself with the Gothic spirit. She was never able to lose the feeling that she was a child of the Twentieth Century trying to express herself in a form that was alien. She had illustrated several children's books when her own book of poems, *Puck in Pasture*, was published by Doubleday, Page & Company, in 1925. This slim volume, which she designed from jacket to end papers, won her such distinction as an illustrator that she was able to devote herself entirely to books.

The lyrics in *Puck in Pasture* are of haunting Irish folk quality as elfin as the drawings. *The Leprecaun*, with its headpiece a moonlit fairy ring and its tailpiece a branch hung with tiny soleless elfin shoes, is characteristic of the volume's Puckish spirit:

> "Oho! The Elves of Ireland,
> They dance so hard at night
>   They dance their very shoes away
> In splendour and delight.
> God bless their Elemental souls,
> You cannot see them for the holes!

"The only Elf in Ireland
That has a trade at all,
   It is the cobbler Leprecaun
Who makes and mends them all.
The shoes they dance away by night
In green and moony demi-light.

   "He is the first of cobblers
And best of craftsmen too.
   For why?—He works at happy things
By gaiety worn through.
God send us each a Leprecaun
To mend the heart of us at dawn!"

The Man Who Got the Call, Captain Spanish who
left his lady mother weeping and the Dublin ladies
sad, is a legend of gallant-hearted wanderlust with
a wistful stanza about the pretty lady, Kitty
Cooley, who is no match for the green-blooded
wench, Adventure:

"Pretty Lady Kitty Cooley,
      Nor your taffeta, nor lace,
Nor your gold can bring him nearer;
You can look into your mirror,
      He has seen another face,
   A White Woman with the Green Blood!
      Captain Spanish leaves you all,
O he's careless, careless, careless,
      He's the man that got the call!"

47

Midsummer's Night, the whispers of Wally and Jane who looked wide-eyed into fairyland catches the mingled wonder and belief of those fortunate children who make playmates of the elves:

"'Wally, what's at the keyhole?'
  'Whist, Jane, whist! Speak low.'
'If someone were outside peering in
  Would we know?'
What's that at the keyhole?
Granny said, ' 'Tis the wind you hear
  Wandering to and fro.'

"'Whist, Jane! What's at the window?'
  'Wally, whistle a tune!
'There's a gay light goes from the old blue plate
  To the pewter spoon.'
What's that at the window?
Granny said, ' 'Tis the tree-low light
  Of an old, old moon.'

"'Whist, Jane! What's by the rose bush?'
  'Wally, it is fourscore
Wee green Riders on snow-white steeds,
  With the Queen before!'
What's that by the rose bush?
Granny said, 'There were Good Folk once
  But they come no more.'"

The success of her elfin drawings in *Puck in Pasture,* as well as the decorations for *Eliza*

48

and the Elves and *Tales of Laughter*, were in a fair
way to labelling Elizabeth MacKinstry as a fairy-
tale artist, when she was commissioned to do the
illustrations for Percy MacKaye's *Tall Tales of
the Kentucky Mountains*. This gave her an opportunity to do a series of stronger, more robust
drawings which were representative of another
aspect of her art. The centaur, the peach rocked
deer, and the decoration for the title page have a
breadth of conception and execution that is essentially masculine. One of the drawings for this
series, which it was decided not to include in the
volume, has an impish naïveté and folk quality
that is irresistible. God, planted with heavy dignity upon a firm white cloud, listens impassively to
Cain and Abel explaining what happened to the
ducks of Paradise. Cain eyes Abel with a murder-
ous glance, and Abel, suave and plausible, drops
his eyes with a self-satisfied smirk. The sleekness
of curls and the general offensiveness of his smug
demeanour make one almost willing to exonerate
Cain for the consequent tragedy.

But Elizabeth MacKinstry has not yet published the book which she wants most to do. She
revels in the robust humour and waggery of the
Eighteenth Century and is familiar with every
shoe buckle and button and ruffle of those exuberant days. The strongest influence on her work
came from that same source from which Fraser
drew so joyously, the gay, flatly coloured old
woodcuts of Randolph Caldescott's picture books

and the prints of the Catnack Press. Another was Walter Crane, the godfather of children's books who "coquetted notoriously," she says, "with Japanese prints and blue willow pattern plates, and set with admirable precision the canon that book decoration should be for a book, fit the shape of its own page and stay flat on it." Indeed, an artist who has a collection of MacKinstry's books, remarks with discernment that the trinity of her artistic creed are Caldescott, Crane, and Lovat Fraser. It has long been her intention to decorate some full-blooded old Eighteenth Century classic in which there would be the opportunity to frolic unrestrained in the field she likes best. But the very richness of choice made it difficult to decide upon a title. The final selection came about in a curious way. A whim of Christopher Morley, who is himself a joyous and rollicking spirit escaped from the same century, determined her year's work. She and Morley were lunching together one day in Garden City, and amusing themselves by planning collaborations of Miss MacKinstry's art and Mr. Morley's prose, most of them coloured by the age in which they are both steeped. *A Book of Baggages*, the portraits of the naughty ladies to be done by Miss MacKinstry and their romances by Mr. Morley; *Pills to Purge Melancholy*, with an introduction by Mr. Morley, and *Words and Pictures to That Effect* were a few of of the titles that were jotted down on the menu. "But best of all is this," said Morley, drawing from his pocket a small edition of *The Journal to Stella*. "This is the book which you should illustrate." Whereupon he explained that he always carried the *Journal*, not only to delight his mind, but to record the daily consumption of his automobile, "Dean Swift." On the blank pages in the back were neat entries in his small black script, recording each drink of gasoline the Dean consumes. So entranced were they with the idea of a beautifully illustrated edition of the diary that they were transported immediately by the Dean to their publisher, who happened to be conveniently near. There they signed the contract for a handsome de luxe edition of this most human and delightful mirror of Eighteenth Century life with an introduction by Mr. Morley, and drawings by Miss MacKinstry. Whereupon the happy artist sailed to the south of France, where she sits in the sun on a balcony in an unfrequented little mountain village and works without interruption.

WILLIAM McFEE

WILLIAM McFEE

A Sailor Ashore

WILLIAM McFEE whose latest novel, *Race*, is a
return in manner to that first tremendous book
which won him recognition, *Casuals of the Sea*,
was destined for a sailor from the first moment
that his young eyes noticed the oil paintings of
ships in full sail and enlarged daguerreotypes of
ancient carracks about to be launched that
crowded the walls of his London home. Lying on
his stomach on the hearth rug before the nursery
fire and spelling out the story of David Copper-
field, the boy knew his first grievance against an
unjust Providence. David was born in a house in
Suffolk and went to live in a ship, while he had
come out of a ship to live in a house.

McFee was born on the three-masted square-
rigger, *The Erin's Isle*, of which his father was
designer, builder, owner, and master. Later, at the
age of six, he accompanied his father on the captain's last voyage on an old tramp steamer out of
Rotterdam, a voyage on which he encountered a
rich collection of human curios, ship masters,
mates, engineers, and fierce ship chandlers in
Cardiff.

During school years, the boy confined his wanderlust to adventures along the docks, prowling about ships with mysterious teak doors and sniffing the pungent odours that poured forth from the stewards' lockers. Later, he spent three years in McMuirland's Engineering Shops at Aldersgate, an experience which he recorded in an amusing verse:

Dear Pater wrote McMuirland's; McMuirland's wrote
    him back:
"We'll take your son with pleasure, Sir, although the
    trade is slack.
We'll make a useful man of him, and (eke) an Engineer,
For the small consideration of a hundred pounds a
    year."
        "A hundred pounds a year, my son.
        It seems a little dear, my son,
        To be an engineer, my son:
        A hundred pounds a year!"

Undoubtedly, the hundred pounds were well invested, for McFee won his Extra Chief's Certificate from the London Board of Trade, his United States Chief's License, and was elected to an associate membership in the English Institute of Mechanical Engineers. At twenty-four, he took a berth as junior on one of his uncle's ships, *The Rotherfield*, and sailed for Genoa. From then until he stayed ashore several years ago to complete *Race* and fulfill engagements for a lecture tour, McFee has lived at sea. The bright little cafés of Tunis, Malta, Port Said, Smyrna, resounding with the babble of all the tongues in the world and glowing with the warm colours of the exotic southern Mediterranean, are as familiar to him as the banana coast of South America where ancient Spanish grandeur languishes in haughty ruins, or the cañons of lower Broadway.

That a busy engineer should find time to write at sea is unusual, but it was during the few hours off duty each day that McFee wrote *Aliens*, *Casuals of the Sea*, *Command*, *Captain Macedoine's Daughter*, and many of his most charming occasional pieces and essays. *Race* was done almost entirely ashore. But, as the last chapters were nearing completion, the lure of open water was irresistible, so he packed his manuscript and a sheaf of pencils in his bag and sailed on a Mediterranean tour with his friend, Captain Bone. Again, when the book was finished, he shipped, on a pleasure trip this time, to renew old friendships in the ports of South America. Living ashore has its advantages for the busy author who has more work ahead than he can possibly do, but there are times when nothing seems so alluring as the throb of a ship's engines and the whip of the wind against her prow as she moves out.

Of late years, McFee has come permanently to port in Westport, Connecticut, but with the pleasant mental reservation that any day after-to-morrow he may be again commuting to the Spanish main or week-ending among the Andes. On warm summer evenings one may find him frequently striding up and down the lawn of his friend the artist, Arthur Elder, smoking and talking, with his one pet, a great tailless Manx cat, astride one of his shoulders. It is an antique house in which the Elders live, New England Colonial, with all the gracious lines and discomforts that distinguished the homes of our forefathers. McFee first bought it for himself, but soon decided that early New England houses were more pleasant to look at than to live in, so he and his vivacious Greek wife, who came halfway around the world to marry him, live in a modern apartment, where he works ensconced in Twentieth Century comforts.

PAUL HONORE

Paul Honoré

PAUL HONORÉ

A Pioneer in Plastic Mosaic

WHEN Charles J. Finger and Paul Honoré began
to collaborate in book-making, it was a partner-
ship of two robust adventurers who had seen much
of the colour and glamour of life. In his woodcuts
for Mr. Finger's books, *Tales from Silver Lands*,
Highwaymen, and *Bushrangers*, Honoré has
caught the spirit of the author's wanderings in
many a far-away place, in Africa, South America,
the Antarctic, across the Andes following the
trail of Magellan from Belen to the Pacific.

Born in a small Pennsylvania town where his
father owned the local mill and the neighbours
were all farmers of various degrees of prosperity,
Honoré's first memories are of spring floods, ox
teams, and impassable roads, while his earliest
dreams were of going to Pittsfield, forty miles
away, a city remote and desirable as the poet's
Carcassonne. Like many an inquisitive boy, his
first expression of the creative instinct was in
mechanical inventions. He and a playmate spent
many intense days building an entirely new type
of steam engine which turned out, sadly enough,
to be very little different from the one invented
two hundred years before by the venerable Watt

57

himself. But by that time the youthful inventor
had turned his attention to a design which sometimes lures him still, a perpetual-motion clock
run by a continuously moving, unbroken series
of marbles. Another early ambition was to own
and manage a zoo containing particularly lions
and tigers, an ambition which has been trans-
mitted in a more practical form to his son York.
This fourteen-year-old lad knows more about
butterflies and animals than most grown-ups, and
he intends to own a horse and fox ranch one of
these days.

Honoré's restless French and Irish blood soon
drove him to seek adventure in a field as
foreign to his environments as the ice floes of the
Antarctic which drew Mr. Finger. He decided
to become an artist. During various peregrinations
of the family between Detroit and Philadelphia,
he studied with J. W. Gies and John P. Wicker of
Detroit and at the Pennsylvania Academy of Fine
Arts. "As I look back on that period," he says,
"my impression is that I was as lazy as hell.
There were so many opportunities which I passed
up, so many possible avenues of study and ad-
vancement from which I profited little or nothing.
Youth is so completely self-centred, so wholly
preoccupied with the phenomena of its own
personal existence. The world goes its colourful,
exciting way at one's very elbow, but youth,
unobservant, sees nothing but himself."

Becoming interested in the gorgeous colour and

highly decorative quality of Frank Brangwyn's work, Honoré went to England with the intention of entering the painter's school, but when the boy called at Brangwyn's London studio, he learned that it had been discontinued. There was nothing to do but go on to Paris. But Brangwyn became so interested in depicting the devastated condition of the Paris ateliers caused by the modern Art revolution that he decided to let young Honoré study with him, school or no school.

So, for almost a year, Honoré worked in the studio of the famous Academician, bringing for criticism such work as he did in his own studio in another part of London.

"Brangwyn's most important influence was due to his utter genuineness and humanity," thinks Honoré. "He forced one out of all finicky ultra-carefulness and artiness. Direct and robust in his own attitude toward life and art, he required of others the development of themselves as human beings without sham or self-illusion."

Upon his return to America, Honoré devoted himself to two types of work, murals and woodcuts, both of which were well suited to his virile style. His best woodcuts are seen in his illustrations for Charles J. Finger's books, whose highwaymen, bandits, and vivid folk people of the Andes made a strong appeal to his imagination. The colour blocks in *Tales from Silver Lands* are considered among the finest in contemporary books.

But it is in mural art that he has pioneered. His

59

introduction of plastic Mosaic, a new medium for murals, both indoors and on exteriors exposed to the weather, has opened a rich new field in architectural decoration. In connection with the experts of the Dow Chemical Company, Mr. Honoré has perfected a cement which will give such smooth, even results that one can use it to make a hair line. It is weatherproof, and as effective for exteriors as it is for interiors. The new Midland County Courthouse in Michigan, which is called by artists one of the most interesting and completely American examples of contemporary architecture, has exterior murals of plastic mosaic, as has the new high school of Highland Park. Other murals by Mr. Honoré may be seen in the S. S. *City of Grand Rapids*, the S. S. *Put-in-Bay*, theatres in Detroit and Cleveland, the architectural department of the University of Michigan, the old Masonic Temple in Detroit, and many private homes. Recently, a group of leading Japanese architects have invited Mr. Honoré to introduce plastic mosaic to Japan.

Mr. Honoré lives in Detroit, where he and his wife, Ethel Kate York, a painter herself, have built themselves a home after the artist's own heart. One of the most interesting features is the living room, large and low with exposed oak beams upon which the friends of the Honorés, when in exuberant mood, have carved whatever fancy dictated. This, the artist thinks, is a happy way of recording pleasant moments.

CHARLES J. FINGER

Paul Honoré

CHARLES J. FINGER

A Modern Sea Wolf

A MODERN sea wolf is what Charles J. Finger calls himself, a robust, gray sea wolf grown pleasantly plump and domesticated, but with the wanderlust still burning in his errant soul. Now he wanders in the none-the-less glamorous and unexplored regions of literature, and through his intensely personal little magazine, *All's Well*, finds many an adventure. But it is the old times, the hot-blooded, dangerous old times that he recalls in his books, *Highwaymen*, *In Lawless Lands*, *Bushrangers*, *Tales from Silver Lands* (the winner of the Newbery Medal), and the new book, *Frontier Ballads*, which he has remembered and collected.

Many are the frontiers that he has passed, and many the folk songs that he has learned on his zigzag way from Willesden, England, to Fayetteville, Arkansas. Born in the English town known as the home of Thomas Hughes of Tom Brown fame, Finger early set out for America. But he did not tarry long. Like many a boy, his imagination was inflamed by Stanley's Africa, so he went to explore it for himself. Later, he wandered into

South America, cruised along the vast, lonely shore of the Antarctic, and satisfied the liveliest of his childhood's curiosities by following the trail of Magellan from Belen to the Pacific. This led to explorations in the Andes, in Tierra del Fuego, and in all kinds of odd, little-known places. Like Borrow, he lived with his fellow travellers, with Indians, gauchos, miners, sailors, adventurers, stoics, fatalists, or children of the sun. They were his friends and brothers. Two of the most valued friendships of this period were formed with W. B. Hudson and Cunninghame Graham, with whom he kept up an active correspondence.

The wealth of folklore that he collected so light-heartedly in the Andes was later incorporated in the beautiful volume of South American folklore, *Tales from Silver Lands*. The days when the rat had a tail like a horse, the rabbit a tail like a cat, the deer a plumed tail like a dog; when the cold-eyed witch of the Cordilleras lured little children with her ball of magic colours, and Cabrakan, the giant, swallowed goats like strawberries, recreated in Finger's vivid words and illustrated with the coloured woodcuts of Paul Honoré, is one of the most distinguished books of the past few years. It was awarded the John Newbery Medal as the best children's book published in 1924. His newest volume of songs from lawless lands, also illustrated by Honoré, is another golden relic of his youth.

But even the most incorrigible wanderers

settle down. Railroading was at that time a continual adventure, especially in New Mexico, and so keen was his zest for business that Finger soon found himself vice president and general manager of a group of roads in Ohio. His activities branched out into the problems of motor-truck competition, the purchase and reorganization of non-paying roads. In short, he bade fair to become a hardheaded captain of industry.

But the leaven was working in other ways. About ten years ago, he began to send stories to Reedy's *Mirror*. William Marion Reedy told him that he could write. *Century*, the *Smart Set* of the old days, the *Youth's Companion*, the *American Boy*, and other magazines began to publish his tales of derring-do. Year after year, Edward O'Brien reprinted his work in his anthology of best stories. Carl Sandburg discovered the ore of which the man himself was ignorant, his wealth of memories of things heard and seen. Cne day Reedy telegraphed Finger to come edit the *Mirror* while he went West. The problems of the railroads held no fascination in comparison with the fascination of words. From that day on, he abandoned finance for literature.

At the time of Reedy's death, Finger was temporary editor of the *Mirror*. With an impulse to carry on the tradition of the man who had left such an impress upon the work of the young writers whom he had discovered and encouraged, Finger returned to Fayetteville, Arkansas, and started his own little publication, *All's Well*, which has continued to be a vigorous and lusty pioneer among magazines. Through its pages and through his tales published in other magazines, Finger has made a distinguished contribution to literature for boys and girls, and for young-hearted adventurers of all ages.

MAHLON BLAINE

MAHLON BLAINE

An Artist before the Mast

"YOUTH and the sea," said Conrad, "glamour and the sea—wasn't that the best time when we were young at sea, young and had nothing, on the sea that gives nothing, except hard knocks— and sometimes a chance to feel your strength." Glamour and the sea are synonymous to so many writers and artists who have spent their youth under sail that one is surprised to note what little magic the sea holds for the latest of her children who has been swept to fame. Mahlon Blaine, the young artist, whose first experience of New York was a punctured head, gained in a Malay mutiny within sight of Coney Island, told his captain about a year ago to look for another first mate for the *West Colma* because he had decided to stay in New York and make his bread—and butter if may be—by his pen and pencils. Twelve months later, he has illustrated three books for prominent publishers, two of them handsome editions of well-known authors, designed especially to feature his drawings; has sold his sketches to such maga- zines as *Vanity Fair*, and many of his crayons to collectors; and has become, in short, one of the most vivid figures in New York's art world. The sea has made him, but it holds no vestige of romance for him. It is the ports—London, Genoa, Port Said, Macao, Hongkong, Pearl Harbor, San Francisco, and all the smaller ones into which a merchantman noses—that have given him his gallery of wicked, twisted faces: Orientals, half-castes, and fascinating disreputables of every sort. And it is the sea that transported him to the best of art schools, the great museums of the world. While his ship was loading or unloading in port or laid up for repairs, Blaine lived in the museums, copying the masters who could give him what he wanted most in colour or line. In the Italian ports he explored the churches and learned of the primitives, or in the French ports, if there was a day or two to spare, he dashed to Paris and put as many hours of work as possible on a copy of Manet's Olympiad. In Japan, he studied with native artists to master their delicate precision of line. In the Congo, he made a collection of African masks and decorated weapons which illustrate their debt to China. In Shantung, he learned the closely guarded secret of making lacquer—but that is another story.

And a second gift of the sea is the opportunity for adventure. It has given Blaine such a rich and vivid experience with human nature in the raw that he has stored away in his memory material for several lifetimes of work, translating it into colour and design. For Blaine attracts adventure

66

as naturally as honey attracts bees. Even his most peaceful days in New York remind one of John Dos Passos' *Manhattan Transfer*.

A mild summer evening and a Stadium concert saw the conclusion not long ago of an adventure that carried him through a score of years and a zigzagging course around the world. It began when he was fifteen, a runaway boy sailing on his first voyage. Blaine's parents were Maine Quakers to whom art was an allurement of the devil. It grieved them sorely that their son persisted in a tendency to draw. He had to hide all of his sketches, but occasionally, when one was found, the parental wrath descended. The final cause of young Mahlon's determination to go to sea was a drawing of the battle of David and Goliath. David was very small, Goliath, very large, and the stone in the challenger's sling almost as big as he. The rooters for David were divided from Goliath's supporters by a line drawn down the middle of the page. On one side were hundreds of minutely drawn Jewish faces, but Mahlon did not know about the racial affinities of Goliath's countrymen, so he made them Germans. He had toiled upon this in secret for many days when it was discovered and demolished, and the loss of his drawing, quite as much as the corporal punishment which followed, drove him to sea. His first ship was a windjammer, sailing from Halifax to Southampton. A day or two out from port, the boy was sent aloft with an old sardine bucket full of paint to freshen up the yellow spot above the black line on the mast. Below him on the deck was a woman who was being shipped by one of the sailors in the crew. Still awkward on his sea legs, the boy overturned the bucket, and the woman received a baptism of yellow paint. Blaine scrambled down from the rigging to be pounced upon by her champion and was receiving a merciless beating from the sailor when the skipper came to his rescue. The sailor suffered such punishment from the skipper that he deserted at Southampton with his woman. There the ship took on new cargo and sailed for Hongkong. As Blaine was loafing along the water front of the Chinese port, he came suddenly upon the sailor, who attacked him with the vengeful memory of their first encounter. But months of sea life had toughened the boy. Although he was no match for the heavy-fisted seaman, he was able to get back to his berth and to be around against the next day. Four or five days later, Blaine and some shipmates were courting chance in a Portuguese gambling house at Macao across the bay. Another patron was the deserter. But this time, Blaine was not taken by surprise and, although he had to stand a stiff beating from his husky opponent, he put up a better defense.

Several years passed. Blaine had revelled in the local colour of many a strange port before he met his enemy again. This time it was in a saloon in Limehouse. Suddenly, in the crowd of boisterous sailors, Blaine saw his old foe and fortunately saw him first. He would not have avoided a fight, but, having other matters on hand, he engaged the help of two Norwegians, who quickly and efficiently removed this obstruction to his plans.

Again years passed. The fourth encounter was halfway around the world. In Pearl Harbor, the two ran across each other and fought a valiant battle. The boy had harder muscles and much more experience in the technique of fist fighting, but the older man was still more than a match for him and beat him with the accumulated venom of an ancient grudge. Time left the sailor still a sailor, but Blaine became a petty officer. Sometime later, as he was shipping a crew in Brooklyn, he saw the sailor coming toward him up the gangplank, but the face disappeared and he was not found among the crew.

This last avoided encounter brings the adventure to its dénouement near the Stadium. Blaine had taken a bus to the symphony concert, but had boarded the wrong one and, trusting to his sense of direction, alighted at some dark cross street near the bottom of the hill. He was walking briskly along when he saw looming toward him out of the dark the face of the sailor.

His first impulse was flight, for the memory of the old beatings rose painfully before him, and a stab on the wrist from a Malay knife had reduced his fighting prowess. But that he would not do. There was no help in sight. No sailor ever calls upon the police, so he put his hand in his pocket and gripped a pipe, hoping the sailor would think it a revolver. The man grasped his arm. "I want to talk to you," he said.

"But I won't talk to you," answered Blaine.

"You must. I have something to say to you." Blaine tried to shake him loose.

"Don't be afraid of me," the sailor's fingers were like iron. "Jesus has come into my heart and has worked my salvation. Are you saved?"

The artist drew a long breath and relaxed his guard. "Yes," he announced with heartfelt earnestness. "I am saved."

He promised to go to the Bowery Mission with his old enemy. The two solemnly shook hands and thus closed the adventure of the sardine bucket and the yellow paint.

Shipwrecks and mutinies were all a part of the day's work. They make good tales for the entertainment of one's friends and Mahlon Blaine tells them with the seaman's delight in dazzling a landlubber, but to him there is no glamour in, for instance, a shipwreck on the Mediterranean, which rivals the one in Conrad's *Youth*. The cargo had been grain carried from the Pacific Coast to the Orient. After dumping it at Malta and shipping a load of barrelled alcohol, the boat put out into the Mediterranean. There was a heavy ground swell and the chaff left from the grain started a spontaneous combustion which ignited the alcohol. Blaine was off watch on the forward hatch when smoke, followed a second later by a sheet of flame, burst through the decks, separating him from the rest of the crew and the boats. He plunged into his cabin, and in that blind moment when the mind acts neither with rhyme nor reason, seized a chronometer which weighed about eleven pounds, a sextant, and his portfolio of drawings. Without taking time to kick off his shoes, he jumped thus loaded into the water. How he performed the feat he will never know, but when he was picked up by the boat, he still had the sextant and the portfolio. The ship was a blazing furnace. In not more than five minutes, it burned to the water's edge. Only one boat had got off, and it was not a lifeboat, but a small one, called a boarding boat, used for going ashore. It was unprovisioned, but they managed to catch a little water from a short rain. For three days, they rowed toward Malta through the heavy swell. A few of the sailors died quickly from their burns, some went mad and were thrown overboard. At last a British cruiser picked them up, and Blaine, with no worldly goods except his portfolio of drawings, landed in Malta to look for another berth.

An adventure of a less tragic nature was connected with another grain carrier, the steamer *Hardcastle*, out of Seattle, commanded by Captain Peacock. Dumping the wheat at Hongkong, they loaded a general cargo, chiefly apples. At Singapore, a buyer of circus animals shipped a menagerie: pheasants, orang-outangs, golden cats

71

from Sumatra, black panthers, spotted cats, and a leopard which was chained to his cage in the potato bin. They took on an extra crew of Lascars, Singalese, Chinese, and Malays. The officers were all white, but the bo's'n and quartermaster knew most of the native dialects. A few days out, during a spell of nasty weather, the leopard broke loose and shot out on the deck. The crew, who were on deck, tumbled below. The officers chased the leopard from the deck to the forecastle where the infuriated cat hid in the apple boxes. The electricity failed, and Blaine crawled in among the boxes to find the short circuit, expecting every moment to meet the blazing eyes of the cat at bay. For three days of rough weather, the animal was loose. The Malays gathered in sullen quiet groups, and the officers prepared for a mutiny. The natives insisted that the cat was a were-leopard, a member of the crew who would materialize at any moment as a human being, one of those super-creatures, at will animal or man, who feed on human flesh. Finally, the leopard was enticed into a net by the temptation of food and was again chained securely in the potato bin. But the Malays would not go near the bin. At the first stop on the Indian Ocean side of the Suez Canal, they deserted quietly and silently, escaping at the first possible moment from the horror that the ship held for them. His own experience with this Malay superstition of gruesome were-beasts made Blaine especially interested in Sir Hugh Clifford's story, "The Were-

Tiger," in *The Further Side of Silence*. One of his most effective decorations in the beautifully illustrated edition of this book is Haji Ali caught climbing into the hut at the moment of his transformation from tiger to human form.

It was in Java that Mahlon Blaine learned to do batiks in native fashion, applying the wax so smoothly and accurately that he could leave an exposed line of linen the breadth of a hair. It is one of Blaine's artistic tenets that the art of a race should be practised in the habitual posture and costume of the native artists. It is his cross-legged position that makes possible the peculiar swish of the hand which is the secret of the native artist in batiks, and it is the Japanese artist's custom of holding his right kimono sleeve together at the wrist with his left hand, thus furnishing a support and fulcrum for his left wrist, that makes possible the clean, smooth Japanese brush line. For craftsmanship, he finds China the most interesting country in the Orient. Some day soon, he plans to return to a certain city in Shantung where the wood carvers' guild does carvings of surpassing loveliness.

During his last voyage to China, Blaine learned the secret of lacquer in a manner that is characteristic of his directness and ingenuity. The great centre of the lacquer-making industry is Ning Pó. It is controlled by a guild of artisans who guard jealously the secrets of the craft. Blaine rented a room across from the large glass-paned building in which the guild worked, and invited a Chinese art student to stay with him. With powerful binoculars, they watched the artisans at work. The first and simplest secret of lacquer-making, he found, was to keep the wood absolutely dustproof. The room was air tight and thoroughly cleaned; then the workmen stripped to the waist, removed the objects that were being lacquered from their shelves, covered with dustproof hangings. The lacquer is applied very hot, and the workmen work slowly, moving nothing but their arms, and brushing the thin liquid in with great, soft brushes as large as teacups. Yellow is applied first, then orange until the beautiful Chinese red is finally obtained after from fifteen to twenty coats. The method was simple, but it was necessary to know the materials of which the lacquer was made. These he learned by copying the Chinese characters on the paint cans of the workmen and having them translated by his Chinese friend.

While the sea was Blaine's great teacher, spreading out before him the treasures of the world, the actual practising of his art aboard a merchant ship had its difficulties. Officers were generally intelligent and sympathetic, but the crew were wont to think that there was something effeminate and eccentric about a sailor who wasted his off hours drawing and his shore leave in poking around museums and cathedrals. Blaine was quiet about his work, but it was impossible to conceal his drawings entirely from his shipmates, so he found

that a hard fist and a fast uppercut were valuable
in compelling respect for art. Many a fight was
waged in defense of the Muses, some of them with
more or less serious consequences. There was the
incident of the pre-Raphaelite lady, a copy of an
Italian primitive and Blaine's first oil canvas. A
jocular sailor applied to her a term which calls
for punishment, and Blaine sprang to her defense.
His shipmates, hearing the row and thinking that
the fair fame of a real woman was in question,
rallied to his support, but their disgust was un-
bounded when they discovered that they were
fighting for a square of canvas. Later, the same
jokester, with the humour of a subway artist,
painted a moustache on the lady. Blaine fell upon
him and threw him overboard, but the ship happened to be in port, and he was fished out by the
crew. Months later, the artist settled the score
by leaving the sailor insensible in a Hawaiian port.

It was at about this time that Mahlon Blaine
suddenly awoke to the beauty of words, to the
music, the cadences, the colour of poetry. He
found a copy of Keats in a second-hand book stall
and carried it about in his pocket concealed in the
yellow cover of a French novel. Somewhere he
found *The Idylls of the King*, and tearing them
out a few sheets at a time, he backed them up on
wrapping paper and kept them in his coat. One
night, while he and his shipmates were drinking
" 'arf-an' 'arf" in a four-ale bar, a roistering,
half-lit sailor pulled these sheets of wrapping

paper from his pocket and began to chant in a thick-tongued Cockney accent the opening lines of *Lancelot and Elaine*. The history of the lily maid did not progress far. In a moment, Blaine had pounced upon him. Soon the whole crowd was fighting cheerfully and quite unconscious of the fact that they were battling over Tennyson. The police finally broke up the *mêlée* and the battered crew fled through side streets toward their ship.

This and many similar evenings spent in the alleys of Limehouse have left such impressions on Mahlon Blaine's memory that he had but to call upon his own experiences for the illustrations in the vivid edition of Thomas Burke's *Limehouse Nights* which is one of the most decorative books of the past few years. The full-page illustrations in black and white are superimposed on a patterned colour plate of yellow, the tone of London fog, and the gleam of rain on wet pavements, the shimmer of street lights in the mist, are effected by rhythmic, broken lines of black that have a startlingly luminous quality.

In *The Sorcerer's Apprentice* he uses another technique. Instead of broken gleams of black and white, he uses a broad reed pen to sketch in a foreground which frames in deep perspective a landscape traced with a delicate pen line. The twenty-odd headpieces to the chapters are as many scenes of a little Italian town, boats and bridges, houses perched on cliffs, and barnyards set far back behind their heavily drawn foreground

76

like vistas seen through trees, delicate and far away.

After Blaine won his first papers, it was his duty to keep his crew out of jail while in port or to get them out by sailing time. Of all ports, Malta was most difficult, for Maltese wine is potent stuff, much like Marihuana. It crazes one, and drinking water makes it doubly effective, giving the drinker two sprees for one. So devastating is its effect that most countries have banned its importation. The jails of Malta are always full of half-mad sailors and officers wearing off the effects of a night's carousal.

On a drizzly evening in February, Blaine's steamer, which had been loading at Malta, was scheduled to sail. All of the crew were rounded up except one sailor who was discovered locked in a one-room jail in a little village on the outskirts of the town. Taking with him several of the crew, and an iron jimmy with a hook, Blaine set out to the rescue. The padlock, a beautiful new one, the size of an alarm clock, could not be broken with the tools they had, so the sailors began to strip off the slats from one of the walls. Occasional passersby loitered curiously and the sleepy policeman on the other side of the square showed signs of rousing, so the crew lifted the building on their shoulders and carried it into a side street around the corner. There, in the light from a chemist's window, they tore away one side and dragged out their unconscious shipmate. But the thought of

tearing down a jail was such an amusing idea
that they finished their work, pulling away the
slats from the side and roof, knocking apart the
framework, and piling the wreckage in a neat heap
in the middle of the street. To add an appropriate
climax, they returned to the square and carried
away the few stones that had served as founda-
tions. These made an impressive cornice for the
pile. The drugged sailor could not walk, and the
only cart was the fire wagon standing under the
great iron hoop across the square from the site
of the jail. The one street light fell directly on it,
so the rescuers half carried, half dragged their
man the long two miles to the harbour. The sailing
was made on time, and the young officer returned
to the comparative quiet of the sea.

But even aboard ship, life is varied. A mate is
often called upon to solve all sorts of unsolvable
problems for the younger boys in the crew. One
bright lad Blaine remembers with special affection.
He wanted to be a novelist and was convinced
beyond the shadow of a doubt that he could write
if he had a typewriter. Blaine thought perhaps it
might be true, so he gave the boy the opportunity
to make a few extra dollars. In a South American
port a typewriter was bought, a ramshackle old
machine that rattled like birdshot on a tin roof.
For several days the aspiring writer sat before it
pounding out "egg" over and over again. Then
Blaine saw that he must take a hand, so he called
the boy to him and said. "The trouble with you is,

you haven't an idea. To write one must have an idea, and if you don't get one before the end of my watch to-morrow night, I'll put you to polishing the brass." The lad wilted. All that day and the next he thought furiously. Toward the end of his watch next evening, Blaine heard a voice, hissing in a stage whisper:

"Mr. Blaine, Mr. Blaine, I've got an idea." The mate answered without turning his head, "Get out of here. Go back down at once."

"But, Mr. Blaine, I tell you I've got an idea!" Adding several seamanly epithets, Blaine ordered the ebullient young writer off the deck, for it would have been worth his commission if the captain had seen him talking to anyone while on watch. When he descended, he found that the boy really did have an idea.

"Now," said Blaine, "fall to and write it, and the first moment I catch you idling in your off hours, you'll polish the brass."

And such strong-arm means of nursing ambition had a certain success, for Mr. Blaine explains with pride that the boy really did have a completed manuscript when they made port in San Francisco.

That such a life as Blaine's must have had its romances, one can but guess, for the artist is reticent. The only one which his friends know is spoken of among them as his Chinese tragedy. She was a dainty little Hongkong girl of fourteen, the age at which a belle of the Celestial Kingdom makes her début. Blaine lavished on her his accumulated pay. He wooed her with permanent waves and manicures and all the allurements of Western civilization. Then he sailed, after the immemorial custom of seamen. When his ship next made Hongkong he learned that the girl's value in the marriage market had been so enhanced by his gifts that she had been purchased for twelve hundred dollars by a wealthy connoisseur of feminine loveliness.

Now that Mahlon Blaine has come to port in New York, he has not found the life of a landsman especially easy. There were times when art failed to supply bread, not to mention butter or jam, and he had to shovel snow. One bitter day, when a workman fainted from exposure, Blaine took care of him, kept back the crowd of curious bystanders, ordered an ambulance, and got the man to a hospital with such dispatch that the boss, pleased with his ability to handle men, offered him a permanent job in the street-cleaning department. After his elevation, he stood by the manhole and swept a clear place for the workmen to shovel the snow. But this ease was short-lived. While working near the Spanish Museum, he spent his noon hours looking at the Velasquezs. One day, he forgot to return to the shovel for such a long time that he found himself out of a job. Those days, fortunately, are over, for his work has won quick and warm recognition. But he sometimes thinks a bit wistfully of that "grand venomous life" of the sea.

SELMA LAGERLOF

SELMA LAGERLOF

The First Woman of Sweden

SELMA LAGERLÖF has been so long associated
with the deep-rooted folklore of Scandinavia that
she herself has become a legend, this grand old
woman of Sweden. Like Kipling and the late
Anatole France, she is a part of the consciousness
of her race as definitely as if she were a long-dead
and canonized national hero. Her countrymen
read and quote her books with a loving sense of
possession, and repeat proudly that she is the only
woman who has won the Nobel Prize for literature.
And well they may, for to the rest of the world her
stories of the Värmland, of Gösta Berling and the
ironmaster's widow, of big Ingmar Ingmarsson
and the farm that possessed him, are regarded as
the very incarnation of the spirit of Sweden.

Although she fell upon an age of stern realism,
of the unemotional viewpoint and calm, grim,
repressed prose, Miss Lagerlöf is a supreme romanticist. She delights in legends of adventurous
cavaliers, unbelievably beautiful women, sorrow-
ing ghosts, and mad love, with the imaginative
child's gusto for fairy tales. All around her was a
wealth of material. Her native province, shut

81

away in its pleasant valleys, was alive with legends
which she learned with her A B C's, but the young
girl who was eager to write had not the remotest
notion that she could use them, for to her they
seemed too familiar and commonplace for fiction.
So she wrote stories of the Sultans in *The Arabian
Nights*, and tales about Sir Walter Scott's heroes,
with results whose lack of originality fortunately
she could not see.

In *The Story of a Story* from *The Girl from the
Marsh Croft*, Miss Lagerlöf tells how she covered
every scrap of paper that she could find with plays
and verse and romances. When she wasn't writing,
she was waiting and dreaming about fame. In
fact, her imagination had pictured the learned and
influential stranger who would one day, quite
by accident, read some of her stories and discover
that she had genius. After that, all the rest would
come of itself.

But the twentieth birthday came, and the
stranger had not appeared, so Miss Lagerlöf went
to Stockholm to take normal training. It was
during this first winter, while the gray streets and
crowding stone walls of the city hedged in her
country-loving spirit, that she suddenly realized
what priceless material there was in her own
Värmland if she had the wisdom and art to handle
it. From that moment, the story of a Värmland
cavalier began to take shape in her imagination.
The original was a fascinating tutor whom her
father knew, a man who "brought joy and cheer

SELMA LAGERLÖF

with him wherever he went. He could sing, he composed music, he improvised verse. If he drank himself full, he could play and talk better than when he was sober, and when he fell in love with a woman it was impossible for her to resist him."

During the next two or three years, two chapters got written somehow or other. After the fashion of the time, she tried to tell her story in the restrained manner of the realists, although she was wretchedly conscious of the fact that there was an irreconcilable discrepancy between the matter and the manner of the tale.

A visit to Mårbacka, her childhood home, for what she believed was the last time—it had been sold and was to pass into the hands of strangers— influenced her to write the book in her own manner with the ohs and ahs and the swinging, almost rhythmical prose that belonged to the glamorous old romanticisim which the world thought dead. There was only an hour or two in the afternoons which she could snatch from teaching, but during these Miss Lagerlöf wrote in a delirium of en- thusiasm the story of the young countess's tramp over the ice, and the flood at Ekeby, of the gouty ensign who wanted to dance the Cachuca, and old Mamsell who visited the Broby clergyman.

When a prominent Swedish magazine, *Idun* offered a prize in 1890 for a short novelette she selected five chapters which were sufficiently well connected, and submitted them. Three months later, she received the prize, for which she

83

had long ceased to hope, and knew that at last she could devote herself to the work which had obsessed her for so many years.

Gösta Berling, although it is a first book and, according to Miss Lagerlöf, "was never disciplined and restrained," remains her masterpiece. Into it she gathered, with the glorious extravagance of youth, the folk tales and legends of the Värmland which were richest in drama and the glamour of accumulated romance. Christmas Eve at Ekeby, when Gösta Berling toasts the devil, and he comes in the flesh to join the party, with horns and hairy tail and cloven hoof, leaning with princely bearing on the old coach box, and lifting the goblet of brandy with clawed hands; the Ball at Borg, and the mad ride with beautiful Anna Stjernhök through the snow forests, with the wolf pack hard upon the sleigh in which the young lovers fled; the chastisement of Count Henrik's bride, the lovely young countess for whose sake Gösta Berling thrust his hands into the great flaming fireplace to save her the humiliation of kissing them; these are the richest essence of romance. And Miss Lagerlöf tells them with the tenderness and gusto, the round-eyed wonder of a child repeating a favourite fairy tale. Indeed, these stories were her first fairy stories, told by her father and Aunt Lovisa and Back-Kaisa, the nursemaid who came from the forest, long before the little girl learned to read. All of the stories were concerned with places about Mårbacka, and a few

of them had to do with the history of the Lagerlöf
family. Mårbacka itself was hoary with legends.
The oldest part of the farmhouse dated back to the
time of the great-great-great-grandfather Morell,
the first master of the farmstead, who was given to
the priesthood by his strong-minded mother, to
lay the ghost of the headless priest who had been
murdered on the edge of the farmstead marshes.
Pastor Lyselius, the great-great-grandfather, who
built the stable for ten horses and the cow house
for thirty cows, not to mention the brew house,
the granaries, and the bailiff's lodge, does not live
in legends, but the next in line, the great-grand-
father, Pastor Eric Wennerick, who married
the dreadful old housekeeper in his old age, and
planted the rose gardens, was the hero of a sad
old romance. In his study hung the portrait of an
early love, a rich and high-born young lady, whose
brother he had tutored. The lovers pledged eternal
fidelity in the bowers of the manor park; but alas,
they were discovered, the young tutor was
promptly dismissed, and all that was left of his
dreams was the pretty face on the canvas. Young
Selma and her brother and sister made a beautiful
image of him, and fingered his harpsichord and
guitar with delight. Then there was the grandmother, once the lovely Lisa Maya, who refused
to marry a clergyman. She was so beautiful that
the young swains would drop ax or scythe and
hurry down to the roadside when she rode by,
to hang over the fence until she was out of sight.

It was she who met the Neckan himself, the river god in the shape of a silver stallion, and was almost lured into a lake that did not exist. Saddest of all was the legend of the whortleberry bridal crown that Mamsell Lovisa wove for the peasant bride when she could find no myrtle, and the fates, as punishment, decreed that her own bridal veil and satin gown should be laid away unworn. All of these stories the children told each other in the big attic nursery under the eaves.

The memory of these days when little Selma, partially paralyzed and unable to walk, was wheeled around in a gay red wagon and petted by Back-Kaisa, are recorded in the informal biography, *Mårbacka*, which is to be the first volume of her reminiscences. The book is in reality the history of the building of a home, for Mårbacka was so permeated with the spirits of past generations who had fashioned it that the dead were curiously real and vivid to the children who lived constantly under their shadow.

It is in *Mårbacka* that Miss Lagerlöf records her own experience with the power of auto-suggestion. The incident is so natural a part of the story that one cannot be sure whether the woman smilingly discredits her child's faith in the healing properties of the bird of paradise or whether she looks upon the episode as a genuine example of mental healing. In either case, it is an unusually interesting story. The child had not been able to walk for months and had to be carried everywhere

86

in the strong arms of her nurse. That summer the family went to the coast to a resort famed for its splendid baths, hoping that the change might help little Selma to recovery. They lived in the home of a woman whose husband was the captain of a ship bound from Portugal with a cargo of salt, and she told the child many stories about the ship. Most wonderful of all was the shining bird of paradise in the captain's cabin. Selma was fascinated with the thought of a bird from Paradise, and although she was too shy to say anything about it, she kept hoping that perhaps it could help her to walk again.

When the boat finally cast anchor in the harbour, Lieutenant Lagerlöf, Mamsell Lovisa, the mother, and the children all went in a boat to visit it. A couple of sailors jumped into the boat and helped the little sick girl to the deck, first of all. Although she had never been on a ship before, she gave not a glance to the mast or the rigging. Her only thought was to find the bird of paradise, which she imagined was as large as a turkey. Just then the cabin boy passed, and she asked him where the bird was. In the captain's cabin, he told her. Giving her a hand to keep her from falling, and himself walking backward, he led her down the companion into a large panelled room.

There was the bird of paradise stuffed, in the middle of the table, and even more beautiful in its brilliant plumage than she had imagined it could be.

Climbing first on to a chair and then on to the table, the little girl sat beside the beautiful creature with the long, drooping feathers.

Shouts from the deck interrupted her adoration. Her mother and father; the captain; Back-Kaisa, the nurse; and all the other guests were rushing about looking for the little girl who could not walk. When they burst into the cabin they asked in one breath, "How did you get here?"

Then the child remembered that she had walked down the stairs. Climbing down from the table she showed them that she could both stand and walk.

Her parents blessed the magic baths at Strömstad, but the child, in her own heart, was confident that it was the bird of paradise which wrought the cure.

The world of the unseen has always fascinated Miss Lagerlöf, whether it be in the simpler manifestation of the old legends, such as the appearance of the evil one at the Christmas feast in *Gösta Berling*, or the vision of the Swedish pilgrims in *Jerusalem II*. The writer's own attitude toward this spirit world is never disclosed. The experiences are authentic to the characters who live them, and this is the only concern of the artist. One of the most tenderly drawn of all her story people is poor Lotta Hedman, the wild little factory girl of Stenbroträsk, who had the gift of second sight and wanted to write down all her visions in plain words to send to the king. Her journey to the Deanery, where she heard the heavenly music, is one of the most convincing accounts of a psychic experience that is found in fiction.

The fourteen-year-old child had rowed across the river on a quiet, sunlit summer evening, to take milk to the Deanery. When she came to the kitchen door, there was no one to be seen. As she stood waiting for someone to take the milk, the girl heard music in the room above; no sort of tune that she knew, but "long-drawn tones like a strong soughing of the wind, and full of sound, and so clear" that they felt as if they stroked her cheek.

As she listened, the child felt as if she were "freed from earth and halfway up to God's heaven."

When the housekeeper came into the kitchen, the music stopped. She set something to eat for the child, because the Dean's mother had been buried that day and there had been a great dinner for many guests.

Lotta took courage to ask the housekeeper who had played so beautifully in the room above, but the woman was so astonished that she could hardly speak. The room above was that of the old mistress who was buried that day, and the piano was at the other end of the house where it could not be heard from the kitchen.

The tears came into the child's eyes, and she was about to run away when the Dean entered and

heard the story. He rejoiced that his mother had
sent him this greeting from the other world, and
laying his hand on the child's head, spoke of her
as one of the chosen, appointed to bring tidings
from the dead to the living. From that moment
the girl felt herself set aside to be one of the
prophets of the Lord.

The dead and the living, the real and the unreal,
the realm of actuality and that of the imagination
are so close in Miss Lagerlöf's stories that they
constantly overlap. And this is one element of their
charm.

When *Gösta Berling* had been accepted for
publication, and a year's freedom to write had
been assured by her friend, Baroness Adlersparre,
Miss Lagerlöf set to work with renewed confidence
in herself and her future. The next book, *Invisible
Links*, was a collection of short stories, based for
the most part upon old Swedish sagas, and dealing,
not with the great folk of *Gösta Berling*, but with
the peasants and fishermen of the desolate Northern forests. So great was its success that King
Oscar and Prince Eugen of Sweden gave her
financial aid, and in the same year she was
awarded a small sum by the Swedish Academy.
Then followed the *Miracles of Antichrist*, the
fruit of a happy vacation in Italy; and *From
a Swedish Homestead*, a volume made up of a
novelette and several short stories, among them
the remarkable one, "Queens of Kingahalla."

In *Jerusalem*, the two-volume work which followed, Miss Lagerlöf accomplished what most artists would have pronounced impossible. She created an artistic story, a book which ranks as one of her biggest achievements, out of the facts which she gathered during an investigation of a Swedish settlement in Jerusalem. In the early 1890's a company of peasants from the district of Dalecarlia had made a pilgrimage to Jerusalem to join an American colony which had established a mission in the Holy City. Grim stories of their fate in the Holy Land and alarming rumours of the conduct of the mission came back to Sweden. "Jerusalem kills" became a saying in her native country that Miss Lagerlöf set out to investigate. She found conditions pitiable. The Dalecarlians, removed from their crisp Northern atmosphere, fell an easy prey to the fevers and the unaccustomed hardships of the heat and the desert. But they held to their undertaking and would not consider returning to their homes. Out of this background of facts, so new and raw in its colours that few novelists would have attempted it, Miss Lagerlöf wrote the work which is considered by many her masterpiece.

The first volume is, in a sense, an introduction to the second, although it is a complete work in itself. Primarily the story of the Ingmarssons of Ingmar Farm, it becomes a mirror of the parish life, developing the interrelationship of the schoolmaster, the pastor, the tavern keeper, and the smaller farmers with the fortunes of the stalwart untitled peasant nobility who made Dalecarlia one of the most solid and conservative provinces in Sweden. The two generations of Ingmars who were torn between love of a woman, and that strongest of all emotions among the peasants of the old world, love of their land and homesteads, are so dramatically and understandingly drawn that, in justification of the breaking up of the community to set out on a religious pilgrimage, Miss Lagerlöf rises to a pitch of tragic intensity which almost reproduces the religious fervour of the pilgrims themselves. The second volume, *The Holy City*, deals with the actual theme which Miss Lagerlöf wanted to handle, the strange fortunes of the Swedish pilgrims at the American colony in Jerusalem, but it would have been far less understandable without the background of life in Dalecarlia.

It was soon after the completion of *Jerusalem* that the school authorities asked Miss Lagerlöf to write a book for the school children of Sweden, a reader which would preserve the traditions and folk lore of Swedish life and teach, at the same time, the salient features of the country's geography. As a result, Miss Lagerlöf wrote two books which have become classics in the child's library: *The Wonderful Adventures of Nils* and *The Further Adventures of Nils*. These stories of the naughty little boy who was transformed into an elf, and sailed north across Sweden on the back of a wild white goose, are read not only by children, but by all those who still "have fairy godmothers in their souls."

In the tale of Nils's homeward journey from Lapland, Miss Lagerlöf tells what difficulties the books presented. She thought about them from Christmas until autumn, but could not write a line. Finally, she became so tired of the idea that she decided to stick to her legends. But the theme would not be abandoned, so she left the dusty streets of the city and made arrangements to go back to Mårbacka, which, although now in strange hands and much changed, held many pleasant memories of her own childhood. The encounter with the elf who gave her the theme for the story is a fairy tale in itself as Miss Lagerlöf tells it.

"As she sat in the cart and drove toward the old homestead, she fancied that she was growing younger and younger every minute, and that soon she would no longer be an oldish person with hair that was turning gray, but a little girl in short skirts with a long flaxen braid.

"She lingered in the shadow under the big mountain ash at the entrance to the farm, and stood looking about her. As she stood there, a strange thing happened:

"She heard a couple of piercing cries from the garden, and as she hastened thither she saw a singular sight. There stood a tiny midget, no taller than a hand's breadth, struggling with a brown owl. At first she was so astonished that she could not move. But when the midget cried more and more pitifully, she stepped up quickly and parted the fighters.

"'I understand that you take me for one of the tiny folk,' said the midget, 'but I'm a human being, like yourself, although I have been transformed by an elf.'

"The boy did not mind telling her of his adventures, and, as the narrative proceeded, she who listened to him grew more and more astonished and happy.

"'What luck to run across one who has travelled all over Sweden on the back of a goose!' thought she. 'Just this which he is relating I shall write down in my book. Now I need worry no more over that matter. It was well that I came home. To think that I should find such help as soon as I came to the old place!'"

It was soon after the publication of *The Adventures of Nils* that Miss Lagerlöf received the first of the two unique honours that have been conferred upon her. In 1919, the Swedish Academy awarded her the Nobel Prize of $40,000 for literature. So far she is the only woman who has ever been so honoured. In the words of the announcement, the award was made "for reason of the noble idealism, the wealth of imagination, the soulful quality of style which characterize her works." Later she was made a member of the Swedish Academy, that group of eighteen immortals which had never before admitted a woman to membership.

The past fifteen years have been full of honours, and the early financial difficulties have vanished. Living in pleasant retirement at Mårbacka, which she was able to purchase from the strangers who had bought it after her father's death, she has written *Liljecrona's Home*, *The Emperor of Portugallia*, *The Outcast*, and the first volume of her autobiography, *Mårbacka*.

But Miss Lagerlöf has not remained remote from the social movements of her time. Although naturally shy and reserved, she became the Swedish champion of woman suffrage; and has been urged many times to run for the Riksdag, the Swedish Parliament, but has always declined because she wished to devote all her time to literary work.

Her home, however, remains Miss Lagerlöf's most pleasant diversion, for the lady of Mårbacka Manor prides herself upon being a first-class farmer. She cultivates one hundred and forty acres, although there are still wide tracts of forests, looks after fifty-three tenants, runs a store for them, and a library, generally supervises their education, and manages the marketing of her farm products; all this in addition to her writing.

Miss Lagerlöf has taken pains to restore the manor as nearly as possible to its condition in her father's time, but she has also made her contribution to its beauty and prosperity. Each succeeding generation since the days of her great-great-great-grandfather has added something to the homestead: stables or cowhouses, granaries, brew house, bailiff's lodge, or beautiful rose gardens. Her own father, Lieutenant Lagerlöf, always dreamed of raising the dwelling to two stories, and even went so far as to cut the timber for the roof trusses. But he died before his plan was realized. Within the last few years, his daughter has remodelled the old homestead in the spirit of her father's plans, and made of it an attractive modern dwelling. Not only has she added another story, making the walls all of smooth white stucco, but she has built also a third story with pleasant dormer windows looking out from the tiled roof, and an additional half story with small oblong windows of its own. The wide verandah and white Colonial pillars remind one of the fine old colonnaded houses of our own South. Although she has installed every modern convenience, Miss Lagerlöf has retained the dignity and simplicity of the original home, and has been especially careful to preserve the fine old trees and the rose gardens.

With her secretary and old friend, Miss Valborg Olander; the housekeeper, who has been with her twenty years; two maids, who have grown up on the estate; Kirre, an ancient black poodle; Pharaoh, the peacock, and his consort; not to mention the horses, cows, chickens, hogs, and bees, Miss Lagerlöf lives tranquilly at Mårbacka, looking after the welfare of those about her, and writing the second volume of the history of her life. Happy in the beloved surroundings of her childhood, she writes in quiet contentment, drawing from the storehouse of her memory stories and themes woven out of the rich folklore of her native Sweden.

CHARLES LIVINGSTON BULL

CHARLES LIVINGSTON BULL.

CHARLES LIVINGSTON BULL

Portrait Painter of Wild Animals

THE animal painter has to know so many more things than painting and drawing that he might quite as easily be mistaken for an anatomist, a biologist or an explorer. And indeed he has to be all of these. Charles Livingston Bull, whose birds and animals are known to every book and magazine reader, is ranked as one of America's foremost animal painters, but he might with equal truth be called a great naturalist. He knows so much about the history and habits of wild animals that he is constantly settling questions of authenticity for publishers. If an editor wants to publish a compelling story about a South American leopard, he asks Mr. Bull about it and saves his skin by learning in time that there are no leopards on the Western Hemisphere. But a jaguar will answer just as well, so the story is saved.

Although he gave early indications of talent with the pencil and, according to fond parents, could make recognizable pictures of all the barnyard pets at the age of four, Mr. Bull was a scientist before he became an artist.

He is a graduate of that famous old institution,

99

Ward's Natural Science Establishment in Roches-
ter, a taxidermy shop which trained such natur-
alists as William T. Hornaday; H. L. Denshaw,
the artist; George H. Cherrie, the South American
explorer; the late Carl E. Akeley, the taxidermist
and sculptor, who did the great African wing of the
Natural History Museum in New York; and Dr.
Frederic A. Lucas of the Smithsonian Institution.
Dr. Ward was a fierce, brusque man whose establishment was a residence and a few other buildings
with an entrance made of the jaws of a sperm
whale. He supplied the best museums in the country, but his art consisted in stuffing an animal
with straw until it could hold no more.

At the time of the World's Fair, Professor Ward
received a commission to install a collection of
birds for the government of Guatemala, and Bull,
a very proud seventeen-year-old boy, was chosen
to go to Chicago and do the work. It was desperate
work preparing the whole collection in two weeks,
but it was a glorious adventure.

Later, Mr. Bull went to the National Museum
in Washington, where he did his first mural, a
painting of a prehistoric *triceratops prorsus*, in
other words, a three-horned reptile that looked
like a rhinoceros, a portrait of a model of one of
Charles R. Knight's prehistoric animals.

When Beebe made his first expedition, a bio-
logical survey of the Barranca Atanquiqui in
western Mexico, Bull accompanied him as the
artist of the expedition. One of his most vivid

memories of the trip is the remarkable feats of the river wasps whom he used to watch in pursuit of their prey. They stung flies quite as large as themselves, and ferried their bodies across the water to their nests, often dragging them over stones that to them were mountains.

It was Beebe whose criticism of an early painting made the young artist determine that accuracy was quite as essential as artistry. He had done an effective design of a snow leopard plunging into a snow bank and startling a pheasant. Beebe reminded him that pheasants were not found within two mountain ranges of that particular kind of leopard.

After leaving the Museum, Mr. Bull found more work than he had time to do illustrating animal books and stories, such as *All Around Robin Hood's Barn*, Walter Dyer's recent story of twenty-four dogs, all of which have portraits in two colours. The hero, Robin Hood, is Mr. Bull's own dog, now six or seven years old, but still frolicsome and active.

Next to illustrations, Mr. Bull likes to do murals. He looks upon his decorations for a handsome camp in the Adirondacks as one of the most pleasant of his experiences. Around the white birch walls of the huge two-story living room, he painted a frieze of all the animals of the region in their natural surroundings. Another favourite work of his is a mural painted in wax colours directly on the wall in a lunette above a fireplace. A flock of pheasants are flying downward into a dull glowing sunset against which are the silhouettes of a few slender trees. Outside the lunette the blue of the early twilight fades off into the pale buff of the other walls.

When Mr. Bull built his own studio in New Jersey, he planned a lunette above a fireplace large enough to hold a whole log, and other spaces well proportioned for murals. That was several years ago, but as yet the walls are in their pristine bareness. He has never found time to put aside his work to decorate his own house. At most, he steals away with his family on a ten-day fishing trip to South Carolina, on a deserted beach where there are letters and telegrams only twice a week. After murals, his greatest delight is Japanese prints, and it is his wife's contention that, when they are travelling, all she ever learns of a city is the location of its zoo and print shops.

ANZIA YEZIERSKA

ANZIA YEZIERSKA

A Pilgrim in Search of a Laugh

LIFE is grim in Hester Street. The fierce struggle
for necessities in the squalid tenements of the
East Side robs children of their happiest heritage,
the heritage of laughter. Anzia Yezierska, whose
stories of the bitterly poor, *Salome of the Tenements*, *Hungry Hearts*, her autobiographical novel,
Bread Givers, and *The Arrogant Beggar* have
dramatized with a certain strong beauty the
sordid, ugly, grinding daily battle of the fishwife,
the washerwoman, and the sweatshop girl, was
not born in Hester Street, but she came to it early
enough to feel its impress on her youth. A Slav
from eastern Poland, an Oriental looking toward
America as the promised land, where such properties as feather beds, *gefülte* fish, and the ancestral pots and pans were useless because it was
a golden country literally flowing with milk and
honey, young Anzia, with her father, mother, and
sisters, arrived in New York. Left behind were all
their treasures except the Holy Torah and the
other sacred books belonging to her father. They
were the light of the world, and in America he
would gain honour and glory for his learning.

From this golden myth to the realities of Hester

Street was a bitter transition to the thin little girl with the blonde braids. "Blut-und-Eisen," the family called her, and blood and iron she was. The girls were the bread givers. Each week they brought home from the sweatshops their wages and gave them to their mother. Sometimes there was enough to eat, but oftener there was not. Rent day was an overshadowing horror. But the father, a stately and holy old man, ate the fat of the soup and concerned himself not at all with such mundane matters as food and clothing for his family. Little Blood-and-Iron rebelled. She determined to pull herself out of Hester Street and to find that America of which she had dreamed. With a magnificent capacity for endurance, she set about educating herself, working during the day in laundries, covering buttons, washing dishes, and going in the evening to night schools. And ever some hidden impulse goaded her to write. For years, she jotted down things that flashed through her mind, a phrase, a sentence, sometimes the middle or tag end of a thought. The habit helped her to forget her loneliness. She wrote these little notes on whatever she could find, the edge of a newspaper or a lunch bag. Then she threw them into a soap box under the bed. When that was full, she stuffed the scraps of paper into the old brown bag that had served to carry the family pillows and feather beds from Poland to America. A rag-bag of dreams, but it was the only real life of the girl who spent so many weary hours in laundries and shops.

But all this time there was never an echo of laughter in Anzia Yezierska's life. The days were too exhausting, the nights all too short to accomplish what she had to do. To be able to see the amusing inconsistencies of the father, whose inhumanity to his own children he reconciled in such an innocent and lofty high-handedness with his burning faith in God, the amusing mannerisms of the boss, the little humorous incidents of the day, argues a certain detachment of spirit, and the girl was too bitterly pushed, too much a centre of the turmoil to see cause for a smile.

Nor were her first experiences with editors any the less disheartening. There was something pathetically humorous about this young girl seething with magnificent, incoherent dreams, breaking into the editorial sanctums of three lofty-browed magazines, which are most concerned theoretically with the case of the poor. One editor sympathetically offered her a volume on the psychology of madness, and another escaped through a back door while she was still talking to him. But the need of finding a medium of expression was so vital to her that she could feel only the heartbreak of the rebuff. At last, an editor saw in her work the dark and stormy beauty, the tragic intensity of her drama of the poor. In fact, he saw more than she had consciously put into the story.

"Do you know," he said, "some of your characters are grimly amusing."

Amusing. It had never occurred to her that there

could be anything amusing about these poverty-
ridden bread winners of her stories. But as the
editor pointed out what there was in her characters that caught his fancy and intrigued his sense
of humour, she, too, began to see dimly that there
might be a light side to the gloomy world she knew,
a gleam of laughter that would help to make it
more bearable. Carrying away with her this
startling new idea about her work, Mrs. Yezierska
began to apply it to herself and her own grim
problems. Perhaps she could find some cause for
laughter in her own tense struggle to make order
out of the rich confusion of her thoughts, and to
shape the stories that were burning for expression.
It was surprising how laughter eased the tension.
What a magic safety valve it was for tired nerves
and overtaxed emotions! And so this indomitable
woman who had raised herself by sheer genius
from the slums of Hester Street to a significant
position among contemporary novelists, deliberately taught herself the happy habit of laughter,
and found in it a pleasant and effective antidote
for the bludgeonings of life.

BORIS ARTZYBASHEFF

Boris Artzybasheff

BORIS ARTZYBASHEFF

An Artist Errant

Two revolutions, a ship that changed its destination, and, perhaps not least, the wanderlust, brought Boris Artzybasheff to New York, but chance had nothing whatever to do with winning his reputation as one of the most effective black-and-white illustrators among makers of American books. This young artist brings from Russia a rich background of tradition and familiarity with the glories of Byzantine art. He is the only son of the novelist, the late Michael Artzybasheff, whose *Sanine* and *The Breaking Point* were translated into many languages, and spent his boyhood in Petrograd and Moscow surrounded by the literary group of which his father was a dominant figure.

But the boy liked least the winters with their long days devoted to school. In the summer he went to the country home in Ukrainia, not far from the little village which is the setting of *Sanine*. Many of the people from whom his father had drawn the characters for his Russian "Main Street" were still living, and the town had remained almost unchanged in a generation. The child, who

saw village life with the interested eyes of an out-
sider, delighted in the mud houses with their
thatched roofs, gaily painted shutters, and walls
freshly whitewashed every week by their indus-
trious mistresses. He liked to see the women in
their coarse white linen dresses and vivid silk
aprons, their full sleeves rolled up on week days
but decorously let down to their wrists on Sundays,
and to watch the church procession, the girls with
sleeveless jackets added to their weekday dresses,
and bright ribbons on their plaits, the men with
their shiny rubber boots and inevitable umbrellas.
There were also sunny days of hunting, fishing,
riding, and vagabonding with a young uncle,
stolen rides on freight trains, and tramping for
days with the true hobo's disregard for provisions.
Always he told his mother about these stolen
expeditions when they were safely in the past.

It was during his school days that Artzybasheff
illustrated his first book, lettering and illuminating
it with all the care that the first mediæval book-
makers devoted to their manuscripts. For a
favourite teacher, the professor of literature, he
made a limited, one-copy edition of an ancient
Russian folk tale about the creation. A part that
pleased the artist mightily was the poet's theory
that the world was supported on three columns
upheld by three mighty whales swimming about
in the sea.

While Artzybasheff was still in his teens, the
revolution came. It was especially bitter for the

father, because he and the other young intellec-
tuals of his day were in a way responsible, and
they were horror-stricken at what they had done.
They could not reconcile their glowingly idealized
peasants with the creatures who burned and
sacked their homes and murdered their families.

Taking service in the fleet that was supplying
Kolchak's army, Boris volunteered as a sailor
making the ports of the Black Sea. On one trip the
ship planned to sail for Colombo, so Artzybasheff
thought it would be an excellent opportunity to
work his way from Ceylon to India and thence to
Vladivostok to join Deniken's army. But the boat
cleared for New York instead, and the boy came
along, thinking that there would be plenty of
time for fighting but one might never have an
opportunity to see America.

After a long sojourn on Ellis Island and an
appeal to the Russian Ambassador—there was
still some semblance of a Russian diplomatic
staff in Washington—he was permitted to land.
Then he looked around to see what one could do
for bread and butter. A Standard Oil tanker
was clearing for South America, so he shipped
on it and set sail for new adventures. But there
was very little time for explorations ashore for
Artzybasheff was determined to come back to
New York with enough money to last while
he found work in the city. A sailor's pay was
little, but it could be augmented while the ship
was in port, by sacrificing the delight of the water-

front cafés and standing watch for his less provi-
dent shipmates at the rate of time and a half
over-time. By careful hoarding he landed in New
York with a hundred dollars in his pocket and a
few more words of English in his vocabulary.

The first job was in an engraver's shop, but the
hundred dollars soon went, and it was very
difficult to live on fifteen dollars a week. With
many trepidations, Artzybasheff asked for eighteen and was told that he was not really worth
the wage that he was being paid. It so happened
that fortune in a light moment arranged a coinci-
dence. On the day that the raise was refused, the
New York *World* bought several drawings. Be-
lieving that his fame and fortune were made, the
boy resigned and walked gaily away to become an
artist. On Sunday the drawings appeared, followed
in the next mail by a letter from the head of the
engraving firm asking him to call. Artzybasheff
had never seen this august person, so he went
chiefly to enjoy the pleasure of being ushered into
the private office. The president, in a long and
cordial talk, disclosed the fact that he had always
been deeply interested in the boy's work and
confident of his success. If he wanted to return,
the old job was his and the question of salary
would be reconsidered. It was a sweet moment,
but Artzybasheff did not accept.

Fortune did not come as rapidly as the young
free lance expected. Finally, he got some work
from a commercial artist and succeeded far too

well. The first drawing was a bottle, and it was such a good bottle that he was given nothing but bottles to do thereafter, large fat ones, delicate thin ones, even hot-water bottles. Gradually, his scope was widened to furniture, but the supreme opportunity, it was pointed out to him, arrived with the order for an underwear poster to be done for a manufacturer who was very fond of golf. The client had definite ideas about composition. The drawing was to show an open window through which one could see a game of golf in progress and a gentleman in the special brand of underwear looking through the window and at the same time showing the buttons on the front of the garment.

Artzybasheff rebelled. Since that moment he has eschewed advertising and devoted himself to book illustration, in which he has made brilliant use of the exquisite fine line, often a white line on black, that characterizes much of his work. Several beautiful books have been decorated by his pen, among them *Roses of the Winds*, for which the initial letters are startlingly lovely white designs on black, *The Wonder-Smith and His Son*, which lends itself excellently to the rhythmical unreality of his treatment, and *Feats on the Fiord*. This dark young six-footer with the gentle eyes has many plans for future volumes, among them a series of illustrations in gold on white and black. But whatever he does will be dominated by strong contrasts and the rhythm and purity of his beautiful line.

A. P. HERBERT

A. P. HERBERT

An English Funny Man at Home

A. P. HERBERT, the funny man of *Punch*, whose nonsense rhymes and sprightly whimsies are not only a joy to Englishmen but, strangely enough, to Americans as well, takes a keen delight in lamenting the woes of the funny man's profession. One of his most moving lyrics in *Tinker, Tailor, The Wise Child's Guide to the Professions*, evokes pity for the down-trodden humorist:

> "Be gentle to the funny man,
>   And if his jokes are bad,
> Just laugh a little when you can,
>   Because he is so sad."

The creditor is at the door, the telephone is ringing, the fire is out, under the table his sons are playing trains.

> "You should have seen him mop his brow
>   And tear his hair and shout,
> 'I will be funny, here and now,
>   But what, oh, *what* about?'"

Yet, however deep Mr. Herbert's sympathy for his craft, a glance at those of his books which have penetrated to America, *Tinker, Tailor, The Man About Town, The Old Flame, She-Shanties,* and *Plain Jane,* gives one doubt that he has had to sacrifice very much hair in search of the re- calcitrant idea. Nor is his life one long struggle with gloom.

In a charming old house in Hammersmith with the Thames at the bottom of the garden, this lithe young Englishman lives with his wife and four children. The fourth, a son who arrived on Empire Day, is "extraordinarily handsome and good," boasts his father, "and the other children are female and very high-minded." "For the rest, I lead a hideous life and very often shave after lunch. I sit down after breakfast and try to be funny. As the morning wears on, I find the serious side of my nature gradually asserting itself with inimitable force, and by luncheon I am ready to write a tragedy," he writes to a friend in America. The rest of the hideous life consists of tennis playing, cricket, flirting with the plot of a novel, writing a play, and sailing in all kinds of weather. The *Winnie,* in which he and his jovial American confrère, Christopher Morley, have explored the Thames, is a sturdy boat that has weathered many a gale. To be sure, Mr. Herbert recognizes that her name is a source of sorrow to the worthy little yacht, but there is a mariner's explanation. "Do not think me so insensible a person that I would deliberately give a vessel of mine the detestable name of *Winnie?*" the skipper protests. "No, no,

I purchased her with that affliction upon her and, though I have many noble names for her in my mind, there is, I believe, a marine superstition against changing the name of a ship, and *Winnie* she must remain."

And Mr. Herbert has tasted also the joys of success as a playwright. Several seasons ago he was asked to write the Christmas play for the Liverpool Repertoire Theatre whose little group of first-rate Christmas dramas tends more and more to take the place once sacred to pantomime. *The King of the Castle* is of the type of drollery and waggishness that delights their elders even more than the children for whom it is intended. Robin and Susan, who buy a thousand stocks and shares (of all shapes and sizes and colours), at sixpence apiece and sell them to the Prime Minister at half a crown in exchange for the secret of a gold mine in Jing, are first cousins to Peter Pan. And the patriotic pirate who suffers from *mal de mer!*

> "But, ah! how short a step is there
> From high finance to *mal de mer*.
> The nation, sir, that lifts a hand
> Against our well-beloved land,
> That race must reckon first with me,
> But *anyone* can have the sea."

But the full-fledged novel of which A. P. H. had actually written the first chapter before he started work on *The King of the Castle* is still his goal.

To be sure, he has forgotten what it is about now, but he is certain it was very good. *The Old Flame*, his book about the amusing experiences of a properly married man on a six-months' holiday from matrimony, is not a novel, Mr. Herbert says. He does not state its class and genus but, whatever its classification, it is funny. The novel, however, is something else again and he still flirts with the idea, sometimes seriously, on those limpid afternoons when it is too warm to play golf or tennis.

J. J. LANKES

J. DeLaukes

J. J. LANKES

Apple Trees and Art

THE ancestral apple tree is really the beginning of the story of J. J. Lankes, the wood engraver, whose prints have carried his fame from a certain little village up state around the world to England, Italy, Australia, and Japan. For it was from the apple tree in the back yard that Lankes cut and seasoned the block on which he engraved his first wobbly wild duck flying over the marshes. The grass came out clean and bold, but his knife would slip on the bird. Yet in spite of the unintentional white cloud about the bill, the little engraving so pleased its designer that he hacked out blocks from other apple trees.

To be sure, Lankes had had art training. At twenty-four, an age at which, he says, "all art students should either be established or fallen by the way," he got his first formal instruction in the Art Students' League of Buffalo. Afterward there were several years of odd study and odd jobs. Before there had been only odd jobs. As a boy, there were paper and groceries and ice to peddle, for Lankes's childhood was like that of many a small boy whose parents cannot quite

117

make ends meet. Debts were his earliest memory,
coupled with his mother's courageous juggling
with them, borrowing a few dollars from a neighbour to meet an emergency, and, after a time of
unfulfilled hopes, borrowing the amount from a
second neighbour to repay the first, eventually
getting a loan from the first to repay the second,
and so on through days and months when there
was never too great a certainty of food. One day
she borrowed from her son a dollar and some odd
cents, which he had earned in various boyish
enterprises, with the promise to repay it before
night. Later in the day, a quarter was paid on
account, but it also had to be reborrowed, and
finally the hopeless little boy was forced to look
upon the transaction as a permanent contribution.

The child's playtime was spent scratching pictures with anything that could make a mark,
and most of his earliest schooldays were employed
in illustrating the blank spaces of his books. It was
in the first grade that he realized for the first time
the general cruelty of mankind. He drew a goat
on his slate, a good goat, in fact, the young artist
was fired with the conviction that it was the best
thing he had done. But a schoolmate saw it and
threatened to tell teacher, so the evidence had
to be destroyed. School was a dreary, tiresome
business, and the only thing about it which Lankes
thinks worthy of including in his *Life and Loves*
is Jenny, the blonde goddess that he worshipped
at a silent distance. For her and not for the class

he illustrated *Rip Van Winkle* and the *Legend of Sleepy Hollow*.

All other books except school books fascinated the boy, and he literally wore out the small parental library which consisted of the Bible, two large books on birds and animals, a hymnal, and a prayer book. One of these, which was illustrated in the manner of Blake, men with long gowns and whiskers, awed him tremendously and probably accounts for his later admiration of Blake's work. "To me," he says, "there is no picture in the world with more poetry packed into it than the first illustration to Ambrose Philips' *Pastorals*."

It was not until his ninth or tenth year that Lankes's art vindicated itself as a solid asset in the business of life. His paper route was in a district infested with gangs of tough boys who made it a habit to hold him up and go through his pockets. On one occasion, a young bandit found a drawing, and his admiration for the artist knew no bounds.

Lankes's first job was mixer in a baking-powder factory, like Floyd Dell's Felix Fay, with whom he had many experiences in common. Later, there were many odd jobs, some ten-hour stints with a pick and shovel. They were no romantic memories, those days of aching muscles and blistered hands.

While he was making mechanical drawings for a patent-office attorney, a physical instructor applied for a patent on a harness contrivance whereby the busy business man could take exercise while engaged in his regular duties at the office. The drawings had to show the human figure, and the instructor was so pleased with them that he asked Lankes to do some drawings in wash for the mail-order advertising. These drawings were never paid for, but they gave Lankes the determination to become an artist. How, he did not know, for there was no one who could tell him how to get a start. He would have given anything to meet an artist, even a sign artist, but the only solution he could find was a correspondence course. Finally, he heard of the local art school, the Buffalo Art Students' League. Two happy years followed. Then to Boston for a year of more study on a very lean pocketbook. There the problem was to get as big a meal for as little as possible. Soon the students knew where the biggest ten-cent bowl of oatmeal could be found, but it was cheaper still to prepare their own over a gas plate surreptitiously hooked to the gas light. There was only one cooking dish, so on oyster nights it was necessary to eat the oysters before one could cook the soup.

Lankes still preserves his book of accounts. For eighteen weeks he had to live on an average of $5 a week. Looking back, it is difficult to imagine what he could have eaten on $22\frac{1}{2}$, 14, and 7 cents a day. His total for one month was $12, which included one theatre ticket.

Among the commercial jobs that came his way,

Lankes has done almost everything, from Christmas candy cartons and Canadian whisky labels to rat-poison containers. At the time of the despoiled apple tree, he was head draftsman of a sporting rifle factory. He knew nothing about wood-engraving tools, but he came upon a small check gouge used in checkering gun stocks. This and the apple wood were material enough. Nights and holidays were spent contentedly gouging into the wood his interpretation of the simple country life about him, the farmer ploughing on a gusty day in spring or driving a tall-wheeled buggy to a white New England church; old farmhouses; old barns with all the marks of quiet, unhurried rural life.

For a long time, these boldly executed little cuts found no commercial sale. Finally the *Liberator* published a series of them, followed by the *Forum*, *Scribner's*, *Vanity Fair*, the *Print Connoisseur*, *Studio*, and *Arts and Decorations*. Soon he found himself on the road to fame.

In 1914, Lankes married, resigned his position in the gun factory, and definitely gave his time to wood engraving. It was an adventurous step, but the two partners found that, by doing without almost all the amusements and pleasures which most people think necessary, they could make both ends come somewhat near together. Under the sign of the apple tree at Gardenville, New York, Frank Lankes, a roving salt who had abandoned the sea for the hills, set up a printing press, and constituted himself his brother's publisher. From this press, at which they worked jointly, came such beautifully designed little volumes as *Lankes, His Woodcut Book Plates* by Wilbur Macey Stone, a delightful item for those who are interested in book plates or contemporary prints. By the time the four young Lankes arrived and there was bread and milk to provide for this little fleet of human dreadnaughts, as their father calls them, he had achieved a certain amount of commercial success.

Abandoning the paternal orchard, the family settled in Virginia, where Buddy, his brother, and two little sisters might play in the sun while father worked in his improvised garage studio. It is not at all the kind of studio that lends itself as a setting for the conventional studio party, but there is a press and room for all the tools that he wants to strew around. Many of his tools look more like ploughs than the dainty ones that are usually employed by wood engravers, says Wilbur Macey Stone, and it is with these that he gets some of his boldest, broadest whites. Here, too, he is experimenting with etchings and finding the days all too short for the work in hand.

During the last few years, Lankes has illustrated several beautiful books, among them Robert Frost's *New Hampshire, May Days,* an anthology of verse edited by Genevieve Taggert, and Selma Lagerlöf's *Marbacka.* For the end papers and four pastoral scenes of this most exquisite of memoirs,

Lankes has sketched glimpses of her beloved
Värmland, of the island where the famous old troll,
Tita Grey, made the pastor fall into the water;
the forest, deep with snow, where the paymaster
lost the money chest; the old barn behind the
sycamores; and Lars of London ploughing on a
chilly spring morning. Simply and boldly composed, they have caught the beauty and serenity
which Miss Lagerlöf saw in Swedish rural life.

Through his exhibitions in Buffalo, New York,
and Boston, and his representation in the permanent print collections of the British Museum
and America's most famous libraries, Mr. Lankes's
prints have won him the distinction of America's
leading wood engraver. Many of his prints are not
now available, but among those that are bound
in such collections as Bolton Brown's monograph
and Wilbur Macey Stone's volume of his book
plates, there are certain favourites which give one
a special keen delight. Among these are: *The
Sleigh Ride*, a sleigh with two horses pulling up
a curve of a white, cold hill; *Church in Winter*,
which needs no other comment than its descrip-
tive title; and, most delightful of all, *Toad*,
three toadstools done in broad white strokes, a
toad in little jewelled gleams of white, and behind
them the delicate tracery of one or two faint
grasses. Then, too, there are the churches and
houses and barns that record the simple, sometimes stark countryside of rural America. In these
he is unsurpassed. But to venture a definition of

Mr. Lankes's work would be a mistake, for he is still in the vigorous early forties, and no one can predict what new fields he may explore or what further beauty may come from the press in his Virginia studio.

C. E. MONTAGUE

C. E. MONTAGUE

A Prince of Grub Street

THERE is a special magic in the great names of
Grub Street, men whose judgments and opinions
and phantasies are discussed each morning at the
world's breakfast table, quoted at luncheon, and
appropriated at tea. In England, C. E. Montague
was one of these until his recent retirement. His
dramatic criticism and leaders in the columns of
the *Manchester Guardian* were largely instrumen-
tal in furnishing both opinions and their articu-
late expression to a large and intelligent portion
of the English people. In America, Montague is
known by a half-dozen books that he has managed to write during thirty-five stressful years of
editing, and by an increasing number of devotees
who find in his work a rich flavour, a stimulant
filling the brain with "nimble, fiery, and delec-
table shapes" like the sherrissack that Falstaff
was wont to drink. *A Hind Let Loose*, a wistful,
volatile Irish hind, a mountebank with words,
who wrote leaders for two deadly rival papers
"locked in endless strife," a travesty on public
opinion so brilliant that it can best be appre-
ciated by newspaper men who know and scoff

at and are bound by the fascination of the press; *Dramatic Values*, a book of essays on plays and players full of the glamour and dust of the playhouse; *Disenchantment* and *The Morning's War*; *Fiery Particles*, a group of short stories which moved Christopher Morley to rank him shoulder to shoulder with Kipling; *The Right Place*, a book of holiday humours, of sun and sky, Alps and English highways, and dear innocent vanities; *Rough Justice*, and *Right off the Map*, these eight are all his books, yet to those who have discovered them, the beauty of their style compensates for their scanty number.

To know Montague is to know his paper, for although this hale, florid, white-haired sport lover, player of cricket, football, and all the games that interest his seven children, did not bear himself toward it as he wrote of another servant of the "M. G." "as an anchorite to his order," he and the *Guardian* were one and inseparable. Ever since that summer of 1890 when young Montague, late from Oxford with a sheaf of Latin parodies in his pocket, asked Mr. C. P. Scott for a trial on his staff and got it on the strength of these schoolboy *facetiæ*, the *Guardian* has been his *grande passion*. He married Mr. Scott's only daughter, with the years became chief leader writer, and identified himself so completely with the paper that it is difficult to think of the two as separate entities. His only absence was the four years of the Great War when he, although past enlistment age, enrolled as a private and saw service in the trenches until he found himself, much to his disappointment, transferred to the Intelligence Staff. Returning to the *Guardian* after his "mental vacation," Montague was caught up again in the strenuous life of the great liberal daily. And he enjoyed his work. To him a political combat was as interesting as a good play, and he was never so zestful as when assailing a formidable opponent. As a controversialist, he was not more apt at meeting a point than evading it, and many a rash layman, forgetting that "Ed. Guard" has always the last word, braved his indignation and was painfully pinked by his pen. Once he bombarded Sir Edward Carson so effectively that Sir Edward vowed he could not enjoy his breakfast unless he had been turned inside out by the morning's *M. G.*

Although his colleagues knew him as an author, it is as editor that Montague claimed their liveliest admiration. It is whispered that each young sub-editor's matutinal prayer carried a petition that he might some day write like "C. E. M.", and frankly boasted that, if one would understand the perfection of polite apology, he had only to bark his shins against Mr. Montague's coal scuttle.

Although he was connected with the *Guardian* for thirty years and was a zestful participant in all the sport and art interests of Manchester, Mr. Montague is personally the shyest of men, the most persistent and successful dodger of publi-

city. One may know him very well without knowing him at all, as far as any familiarity with
the details of his daily life is concerned. He lives
quietly at one of those long, mellow English
addresses which roll so pleasantly off the tongue,
as quietly as one may with seven vigorous sons and
daughters, playing games with any of the young
people he finds about the house, and struggling at
odd moments with a long novel that is being
whipped into shape. Of his hobbies, he talks with
the same delight that animates his books. Maps
are his passion, and contour lines go to his head.
One has but to read the chapter in *The Right Place*
on "the contour lines that sing together like the
Biblical stars" to understand his delight in old
hill-shaded maps of Derbyshire with their tracts
of high light along the ridges, and the 150,000 Bar-
bey maps of Switzerland which he thinks the most
glorious representation ever given of mountainous
land.

Precision and speed in map reading, as in
reading of a musical score, can be carried further
and further. "Soon," he says, "the map is read,
not word by word, but phrase by phrase; the
meaning of whole passages of it leaps out; you see,
with something like the summary grasp your eye
would get of the actual scene, the long façades of
precipice and hanging glacier that there must be
where the blue contour lines crowd up closely together right under a peak of twelve thousand feet,
with a northern exposure, and also the vast, gently

sloping expanses of snowfield below, where the
lines flow out wider and wider apart, expressing
broad shelves, and huge, shallow basins hoisted
on upper floors of the mountain."

As one might easily guess from his interest in
maps, another hobby is Alpine climbing. Each
vacation finds him in some remote Swiss hamlet
undiscovered by tourists and connected with the
world by no broader road than a mule trail.

Here he scrambles up stiff trails to his heart's
content or sits at the edge of a sunny Alpine
meadow and pencils amusing reflections about
man and his ancestors or histories of single-minded
mountaineers, who "live on from moment to
moment by early man's gleeful achievement of
balance on one foot out of four, or hang safe by a
single hand that learnt its good grip in fifty
thousand years of precarious dodging among forest
boughs with the hungry snakes looking up from
the ground for a catch like the expectant fieldsmen
in the slips." "The Hanging Garden Gully,"
the tale of the modest botanist named Darwin who
changed his first name from Charles to Thomas
lest he should seem to be preying any more than
need be on his hero's honoured name, is a pæan to
the joys of mountain climbing that would make
the most indolent idler grasp an alpenstock and
seek a crag.

But mountaineering and map-reading are by no
means Mr. Montague's only pleasures. When he is
not taking his youngest to a league football match

or the police sports on the University athletic
ground, he may generally be found applying a
highly intensive form of cultivation to the few
square yards of soil which constitute the garden,
and which by such assiduity alone can be induced
to grow some of the hardier sorts of shrubs and
plants. His zest in all kinds of sport (except shoot-
ing and fishing) is that of the typical Englishman
who plays for the game's sake, seldom attains
remarkable excellence in any one, and can get ex-
cited about the last point of decimals in a bowling
professional's average. All forms of bodily exercise
appeal to him, even bicycling, and it is a family
legend that he once rode from Manchester to
London, in one day, for the fun of it. He still
plays the garden variety of tennis, golf, cricket,
football, or anything else that can be improvised
with such members of his family as may be at
home, and their friends. And, physically, he plays
these games with more energy than most men who
are fifteen years younger.

The Montague home is the gathering place for
a clan of young friends and cousins, and at holiday time is the scene of continuous and whirl-
ing festivities. Writing Christmas greetings to an
American friend, Montague says:

"We wade all the morning in brown paper that
has wrapped Christmas presents till breakfast
time and then start again on a grander scale at a
midday feast for my editor's twenty-two descen-

dants. For the next two or three days the Welt-schmerz will be wringing the vitals of all the younglings, but, of course, it's worth it."

Yet in spite of this miniature world that over-flows the substantial stone house with its vine-covered doorway, Mr. Montague's work hours in his study are inviolate. Nobody knows how he allocates his time in this quiet room lined with volumes that pertain in about equal proportions to the theatre and mountain climbing, but his friends make a shrewd guess that it is rigidly allocated according to plan.

Montague is not a great reader, partly from force of circumstance, but much more likely from preference. He confesses that he never read a book when young if he could avoid it. His youth was joyously devoted to all the outdoor games and sports by which study and indoor sports could be kept off. But as his father and eldest brother (now Professor of History in the University of London) read everything and talked about it, the boy was attracted by things that they quoted, and these often come into his head now, ready for use, and gain him false credit, he protests amusedly, for having read books that he never opened. This habit of not reading, he professes, has gained him a great deal of inestimable leisure for mountain-eering and all sorts of ball games, as well as simple repose. If one reads very few books, nearly every-thing in those few seems so novel and curious that it sticks in the mind and recurs amusingly when one is trying to write things one's self. Of course, it is well that one's few books of reading should not be quite bad, he agrees. The first books he read as a child were *Robinson Crusoe* and a good Eighteenth Century English translation of *Don Quixote*, and so he took an early dislike to bad writing, almost as much as if it were bad rowing or bad cricket.

Technical training for literature came from another source. As a boy, he had the good luck to go to a mediæval public school where the education (chiefly in doing Latin verses) was then, probably, almost exactly the one that Shakespeare and the other boys had at the Stratford-on-Avon Grammar School. For ninety-nine boys out of a hundred, nothing, perhaps, could be worse. It was fantastically useless to all the little predestinate lawyers and bankers, but fine for the few who like playing with words.

At Oxford Montague discovered a second alternative to regular work in the writing of prose parodies in the *Oxford Magazine*, in which "Q" (A. T. Quiller-Couch, now the English Literature Professor at Cambridge) was then doing the same thing in verse. These were the juvenilia which won him a place on the *Guardian's* staff.

Youth was for other things than reading and study. Montague looks back now with tenderness toward those glamorous years, wasted as they might seem to the unwise on rowing and any games

and divagations from the highroads, but really the
youth of a *dévot*, "a serious non-waster of sunshine, a conscientious unblasphemer of leisure and
the Thames-side inns and the cricket fields of
Dorchester and Islip and the other clearest mani-
festations of God." His father's home was on the
Thames, and he can hardly make out how his
children grew up right in such a riverless place as
Manchester.

Like all Englishmen, Montague believes that
water is the stuff to be on or in or by. We speak
of him as English, but, of course, he is Irish, at
least, half Irish. He is one of those of whom he
speaks in the introduction to *A Hind Let Loose:*

"Some of us writers have in our veins the Irish
blood mixing uneasily with the English. Descended
from a hundred cats, and also from a line of dogs
equally long, we have been placed by birth behind
the scenes, completely and terribly behind the
scenes, of the cat-and-dog life long led by these
two amiable peoples. There comes to us a sad,
sure, intimate sense that behind all the fine, firm
bow-wowing on the one side and the staunch, intrepid spitting and swearing on the other there
lurks a certain modicum of bunkum as well as of
reason. The full, happy blast of partisanship is
denied us by Nature. The power of hot, uncritical
assent to any blatant squeal of spite, so long as it
comes from the one loved quarter, is not vouch-
safed to us."

But, in the English press, the Irish and the English have learnt most harmoniously to eke each other out. John Bull, publicist, and Shaun McGrath, the lean exile from Erin, are richly interdependent, says Montague.

"John, a man of slowly and majestically moving mind, is sadly prone to splutter, choke, and become unimposing when fate calls upon him to find, at short notice, lofty utterance for one of his own profound dislikes or ardent desires. How different Shaun! Erin herself is as likely to run short of rain as Shaun of apt and eloquent words. Shaun's only worry is lest these facile showers of his should find no crop to water—of course, upon satisfactory terms. Clearly the two men were made for each other, the man with the fine flow of words to his pen, but no topic at all, and the man with the grand things to say if he had not aphasia."

Perhaps it is the English heritage in a perpetual struggle with the Irish that makes Mr. Montague such a slow and deliberate writer. Words, the right words, perfectly attuned to his sensitive Irish ear, are not to be met with casually, but to be wooed and sought after and pursued with single-minded devotion. The sub-editors, who bought his office to refer to him everything that related to Shakespeare, Sunday games, Styhead (and all other passes), road hogs, and the Alps as well as the various political and civic questions in which he was interested, generally found him with his ear turned in abstracted attention to their comments while his pen was poised in the air seeking for the just word to complete a phrase.

At present Mr. Montague is working upon a novel which is already blocked out and is now in the final stages of revision.

"I struggle with this intractable novel "he writes to an American friend," sometimes curling its charmless tail and sometimes sharpening its amorphous snout, and anon striving to breathe life into its dead waist and middle. I hope you don't find that in this sort of statuary you first have to lay down a quarry of solid words and then cut the thing's figure out of it by vasty labours of clipping off and rejection, till the original intention is—or isn't—disengaged from the preliminary verbiage. I can't think anyone ever had a worse method, unless it was Andrew Lang, who had a different book going on in every room of the house and wrote according to where he was at the time and always got late with his reviews for the *Manchester Guardian*, because, we think, he did 'em in the bathroom."

Yet with all his occupation with writing, and the sports of his children, Mr. Montague finds time to help manage a university. Sometimes he may be seen at clubs, and he has even been known to speak at public dinners. But this is very unusual, for in modesty it might almost be said that he is guilty of excess. As for careers, he is much more interested in his sons' than his own. It is with pardonable pride that he speaks of the oldest boy's exploring in Spitzbergen with his Oxford gang and his plans to live in Central Africa and make war on the tsetse fly, or his second son's steeple-chasing for Great Britain in the Olympic games. They, he insists, are the distinguished members of the family.

Of literary enthusiasms, Mr. Montague has many. First of all, is Shakespeare. He is no pedant, but he has joyed so long in the lines of the Swan of Avon that the characters and situations of the plays are as familiar a part of his memory's furniture as the impressions of actual life. Conrad is another. With his friends, Muirhead Bone, the etcher, and his brothers, Captain David of the Cunard Line, and James, the London correspondent of the *Guardian*, Montague has celebrated the magic of the great romanticist's tales on many occasions. "There must be some good in this nation that anyone so quick to scorn justly as Conrad should not have disdained to take it up when he was short of a country," he commented to a friend shortly after Conrad's death. Among Americans he finds a kinsprit in Christopher Morley. *Religio Journalistici*, Mr. Morley's strange and fascinating little book about God in the life of a work-a-day journalist, he found absorbingly interesting.

"It's exciting," he says of it, "to find out that at many odd moments one has been religious, whatever all the raging Mullahs of the sects may say to the contrary, and that one has probably felt, for those moments, pretty much in the way that a fellow like St. Francis feels all the time. Though, of course, one may then be no better than one should be for the next month. I guess there are some fine books to be written about the relation of the religious exaltation to that of artistic creation, that of sex (at its best), and that of liquor (at its ditto). Meanwhile I'm dead sure religion is coming in strong at the queer moments when whole tracts of stuff suddenly show up clear, as they didn't do before, or when something or other is suddenly seen as the one thing to be done, no matter what very good reasons there may be against doing it."

When it comes to philosophy, one can find no more vivid and whimsical paraphrasing of Socrates than that of Sergeant Boam in *Fiery Particles*, when his soul was irrigated by the golden liquor that Farrell made at the edge of the bog, no common sour mash that "would blister half of the lining off the inside of an ass," but the very mellow soul of whisky that seemed to be honey and warm sunshine embedded in amber and topaz.

"Aye!" stammered the sergeant. "Every man has a pack of old trash discommodin' his soul.

Pitaties and meal and the like—worked up into flesh on the man. An' the whole of it made of the dirt in the fields, a month or two back! The way it's a full barrowload of the land will be walking on every two legs that you'd see shankin' past! It's what he's come out of. And what he goes back into being. Aye, and what he can't do without having, as long as he lasts. An' yet it's not he. An' yet he must keep a fast hold on it always, or else he'll be dead. An' yet I'll engage he'll have to be fighting it always—it and the sloth it would put on the grand venomous life he has in him. God help us, it's difficult."

"Grand venomous life," the joy and the zest and the relish of it, that is the characteristic essence both of Mr. Montague's books and of the bronzed, vigorous, white-haired man who, whether he is at work or at play, brings a keen capacity for enjoyment to the daily adventure of living.

JAMES G. DAUGHERTY

James Dougherty

JAMES G. DAUGHERTY

Interpreter of the American Spirit

ALTHOUGH he has retired to Westport, where all good artists go when they leave Greenwich Village, he is known as Jimmy Daugherty around Fourteenth Street, where the legends that he created still flourish. He may sign James G. to the murals which have won high distinction, some of them at the Sesqui-centennial Exhibition, and to the books which have been illustrated by his vigorous pen, but there is an inevitable fitness about "Jimmy" to those who are familiar with his lean young face and Irish smile.

Some thirty-odd years ago Jimmy Daugherty migrated at a tender age from North Carolina, his birth state, to southern Ohio. On the rich bottom lands of the Ohio River, he grew into boyhood, playing hooky at the swimming holes and fishing in the trout brooks that were within tramping distance of the little town. Water, if it were no deeper than draft for a flat-bottomed boat, lured him always, and the docks and water fronts are his most vivid recollections of his later acquaintance with seaboard towns. One apple orchard through which a brook dawdled in the spring under bran-

ches of pink bloom was to the boy the loveliest
spot on earth. Years afterward, he returned to the
village to find again some of the places that had
held a special beauty for the child. They were
nowhere to be found. For two or three hours he
explored the dingy, ugly little town without discovering a single place that resembled even
remotely the scenes of his gilded memories.

In his teens Daugherty lived in Washington,
where the Corcoran Gallery and the excellent art
school gave him a first impetus to art. The city
itself, in the old days before the war and the
outbreak of emergency government buildings
and apartment houses, was a mellow background.
He liked the red-paved streets and the dignified
red brick houses, the little green squares with their
Japanese magnolias fantastically white under the
moon, the towpath where an occasional mule
pulled a lazy boat through the canal, but best of
all he liked the markets. Often the boy's father
walked with him through the stalls, early in the
morning when the country freshness was still on
the vegetables and flowers, pointing out to him the
interesting types that thronged the stalls. The
Negroes with their rolling yellow eyeballs and gold
rings in their ears were a barbaric splotch of colour
sitting among bunches of wild flowers, sassafras,
and crimson clover.

His father was one of the strongest influences in
Jimmy Daugherty's life. Not far enough removed
from the pioneer to take for granted the beauty

of the classics which one learns at college, he read
Shakespeare to his children as if the plays were
favourite fairy tales or contemporary best sellers,
and a worn copy of *The Canterbury Tales* was
generally to be found within reach of his library
chair. He recognized the boy's talent and kept him
steadily at work during those periods of youthful
depression when gold mining or circus riding
seemed more alluring than the difficult road to art.

When Mr. Daugherty was sent by his government on an agricultural mission to Europe, Jimmy
accompanied his father and spent several happy
and more or less profitable years in England
and on the Continent. In London he fell under
the spell of Frank Brangwyn, whose lusty pirates
kindled his admiration, and worked in the Brangwyn studio. Later, he studied in Paris, but one
must not take the words "work" and "study" too
literally, for they meant chiefly "play," he says.
Too definite an influence of European masters was
not an unmixed blessing, he learned, for it took
several dissatisfied, groping years after his return
to find himself and discover just what was the
genuinely American spirit that he must interpret
if his work was to have the sincerity and deep-
rooted homogeneity which true art must have with
the race which produces it.

Settling in New York, Daugherty found a studio
on Fourteenth Street. For him the city was the
Bowery, the Village, and the water front, especially
the docks where the freighters landed their crews,

a fascinating motley from all corners of the earth. His first job was to illustrate a poem, titled *The Breadline*, for *Appleton's Magazine*, long since defunct. It was a grimly realistic breadline that he drew, for he knew it well. The dismal school of art was then at the height of its vogue, and when Daugherty saw his first drawing in print, he was convinced that his mission was to interpret the miseries of the world. Fortunately, this school soon waned, and the young artist turned to happier themes.

Daugherty's next move was to Brooklyn. On top of a factory on the water front were two or three ramshackle studios. The section has been reclaimed since for fashionable studios, but then it was the playground of drunken sailors and hold-up men. Four other artists, an Austrian, an Englishman, an Italian, and a Dane, lived in the building. On summer nights they sat on the roof where the lights of the East River spread out in a fan to the harbour, and the skyscrapers on the Battery were pricked out of the black by thousands of golden squares. Sometimes the Italian raised his voice above the humming of the bridge and sang the lusty peasant songs of his race. Often they talked, these men of so many different nationalities and modes of thought, about that which was common to them all, art and its relations to life. One of the most pleasant features of the neighbourhood was the greengrocer on the corner. When funds were low, a not infrequent condition, he provisioned the little group. And his golden-hearted paternalism toward them was all the more remarkable because, unlike Cyrano's pastrycook, he had not the remotest interest in art.

Marriage parted Jimmy from the harbour and the studio under Brooklyn Bridge, but the Daughertys' first home was in a little Jersey town with a front door on the Hudson. Later, they lived in one of the houses on Turtle Bay, where the corners of pink cement floors and ceilings were rounded and house-cleaning was reduced to a wash down with the hose. Daugherty rather liked the idea of life reduced to such simple mechanical terms, but his wife, who is a writer and, he says, the classicist of the family, held out for the charms of tradition, so they now live on the outskirts of Westport, where much of the simple grace of old New England lingers in the green-shuttered white houses, the tree-shaded streets, and the ox-cart that occasionally rumbles past the door.

During the war, Daugherty served in the camouflage corps making designs for the merchantmen anchored in the harbours of Newport News and Baltimore. The scientific application of the optical illusion which enabled the camouflage artists to reverse the apparent direction of a boat by lines of paint was a fascinating art, developed for the emergency, and now, he thinks, lost to the world.

Since the war, his work has won Mr. Daugherty distinction as one of the outstanding mural painters in America. But he takes a special delight in book illustration, in which the artist finds a pleasant relief from the usual commercial restrictions. In his drawings for Stewart Edward White's *Daniel Boone, Wilderness Scout*, Mr. Daugherty expressed the gusto, the colour, and continual adventure of pioneer life in the Kentucky and Carolina mountains with a vigour and distinction of line that made the book one of the most beautiful examples of fine book-making that appeared during the year, and his forthcoming *Knickerbocker's History of New York* recreates with the same delight and understanding the New Amsterdam of Washington Irving.

Daugherty believes that American artists have begun to awaken to a national consciousness, and that we are on the threshold of a vigorous new native art of which book-making is a part. Indeed, the distinguished books that have been decorated by his pen may well be a strong contributing influence toward such an end.

MARY BORDEN

MARY BORDEN

A Sophisticated Observer

AMONG that younger generation of English
women writers who have raised the craftsmanship
of the subjective novel to a plane that is the wonder and despair of other nations, two are Americans, Anne Douglas Sedgwick and Mary Borden.
And it is not unnatural that both should be
interested primarily in the psychology of race, the
clash of custom with custom and national temperament with foreign mode of thought. Miss
Borden is particularly concerned with comparing
and contrasting national attitudes toward life.
Of her five novels, two, *The Romantic Woman* and
Jane—Our Stranger, are built about this theme,
as is her latest one, *Flamingo*. It is this sense of
drama in the clash between the exuberant ideal-
ism of the new world and the ageless repressions
of the old that led Storm Jameson to call her one
of the most disquieting of modern novelists—
having in an extravagant degree the contrasting
qualities of primitive emotion and mental subtlety.

"She is barbaric" says Miss Jameson, "and rawly
vital under a guise of exquisite sophistication of

145

phrase and manner. She assaults our emotions but not directly; the assault is conducted through the intellect, thus doubling the force of the shock and making an impression infinitely vivid and inescapable. She is cosmopolitan and an alien by virtue of her genius in all three, a dreamer, too clear-sighted for comfort, passionate and urbane, savage, and *merveilleuse*."

The elements of Miss Borden's style, which Miss Jameson characterizes as "raw vitality" and "exquisite sophistication," are but a natural reflection of the author's own life. Like Jane and the Romantic Woman, she belonged to the West. She was as eager a young romanticist, as absolute and unworldly wise an idealist as either of her heroines when she was plunged into one of the oldest, most arrogant, most sophisticated, custom-ridden, and, in its way, attractive castes in the world: the British Army set. The sensitiveness to other people's mental attitudes, which enables her to see both their absurdities and their charms and to analyze with such accuracy her own reaction to them, is the quality which makes her studies of the French equally vivid and psychologically true.

Although, since her marriage to Brigadier General Spears nine years ago, Miss Borden has lived in France and England with occasional visits to the United States, she still has an extraordinarily strong feeling of belonging to America, particularly the West. Her childhood in Chi-

cago and holidays at the family homestead in
Indiana left deep impressions upon which she has
drawn in several of her books. The ample old
farmhouse in Indiana was the scene of many a
jolly Thanksgiving. It belonged to the grandfather, John Borden, a Rhode Islander who in his
adventurous youth sailed down the Ohio in search
of silver mines. He found no silver, but very good
farm land, so he settled on the borders of Kentucky and Indiana and built the friendly old
homestead which his grandchildren made a place
of delightful memories. William Borden, the son,
however, did discover silver. Sent West by his
father and Marshall Field, the founder of the
family, he was one of the builders of Leadville.

Her father was one of the strongest influences
in Mary Borden's life. Several years of study in
Heidelberg had given him a profound philosophi-
cal outlook. He was widely read and had a quiet
dignity that was to the girl a constant inspiration.
In the early pages of *The Romantic Woman*, she
has drawn an excellent picture of him.

He was a reserved man who moved through
life erect and square-set, making about him a
definite silence that it took all of a little girl's
courage to break, but when he smiled, he startled
one with the warmth and directness of his gaze.
Always there was about him a grand simplicity.
His mind was full of knowledge "carefully gathered and fastidiously selected," and the dignity
of his manner was the unaffected expression of his

147

personality. Throughout *The Romantic Woman*
Joan's father played a dominating, steadying
influence in her life much as Miss Borden's own
father did in hers.

In fact, Joan's childhood in Chicago, the games
she played, and the battles between the Hot Push
and the Micks are largely biographical. The Hot
Push was a gang of gentlemen's sons, augmented
by their sisters and their sisters' chums who went
to a private school next door to the public school
and waged daily warfare with the "Micks," who
were dismissed at the same time. There was
constant dispute as to the "right of way" to a
German bakery several blocks distant. The
"Micks" fought to deprive the "softies" of
pumpkin pies, and the "softies," who were a fairly
good match with their fists, engaged in many a
drawn battle. The vacant lots were the fields of
glory until a cry of "the copper" scattered both
gangs into the alleyways. These little pictures of
the gang; of the hundred and fifty white mice in
the attic; of Joan and her chums, three long-legged
little girls in sweaters and tam o'shanters in the
butler's pantry eating devil's food cake and talking
about their destinies, are among the most vividly
remembered passages in that wise young story of
romance and disillusionment. There were skating
parties, too, and bob-sleighing in the winter. The
chief emotional interest was the revival meetings
of the Moody Church. Most Chicago families of
the 'nineties were deeply religious, and it was not

unusual for children to attend the services of some
of the more violently evangelical creeds and to
experience emotional upheavals which they mis-
took for religious experiences, upheavals which
left a powerful and disquieting memory. Mary
Borden has never been able to free herself from a
distaste amounting to horror for any form of
emotionalism in religion.

At fourteen Miss Borden went to boarding
school in New York and later to Vassar College.
There, in common with many of her schoolmates,
she reacted violently to most of the older generation's modes of thought. It was a sign of intelligence to be an atheist, and there was much talk
about free love, trial marriage by five-year con-
tracts, and many another similar panacea for the
ills of the social system.

After graduation and a trip around the world,
she led a pleasantly nomadic life, chiefly in France
and England. The war found her in France, and it
is these four years that she will probably look back
upon as the most intensely interesting period of
her life. She organized and ran a large field hospital
for the French Army. After the Armistice, she
found herself the possessor of five war medals,
the Legion of Honour, the Croix de Guerre, the
French gold medal of the Service de Santé, and
two British war medals.

Her familiarity with the French *haute monde*,
not only with the pleasant social customs of their
drawing rooms, but a much deeper familiarity with

their class and racial modes of thought, her insight
into their mental processes and her ability to
suggest the psychological background which
makes them understandable, is the power of her
second novel, *Jane—Our Stranger*. This is not a
pleasant story. So deftly and impartially are the
characters drawn with all their inevitable antago-
nisms that one lays the book down without
knowing whether he feels greater pity or annoy-
ance toward Jane for her bleak inability to make
any sort of adjustment with French life. Philibert,
with his clever, jaunty little body, his exaggerated
elegance, his cold blue eyes, and his impudent
charm; his mother, the exquisite old marquise who
belonged to the Grand Chevaux de Lorraine and
"was reputed to be the only woman in Paris who
could refuse an invitation to dinner in the same
house six times running without making an enemy
of its mistress"; Claire and all the aunts and
uncles and cousins who moved in a world "exquisite and sterile, beautifully still as a sealed room
with panelled walls inhabited by wax figures,"
Miss Borden brings to life with an impassioned
clarity. And Bianca is one of the most alluring
villains in contemporary fiction. Philibert, who
is thought by many to be modelled on Count Boni
de Castellaine, despised humanity.

"It exasperated him to tears. Its stupidity put
him in a nervous frenzy. He was animated by a
kind of rage of mockery. Everything that human-

ity cherished was to him anathema. He had been born with a distaste for all that men as a rule called goodness, and was nervously impelled towards that which they called evil. And yet the evil he courted didn't do him any harm. I mean that it didn't wear him out or spoil his digestion or stupefy his intelligence. On the contrary, it agreed with him. He had begun to taste of life with the palate of a worn-out old man. The good bread and butter and milk of the sweetness of life was repulsive to him and disagreed with him. He could live to be an hundred on a moral diet. that would have killed in a week a child of nature. Sophistication can go no further."

And Bianca, who had been the idol of Paris ever since she was a little girl, when strangers were taken to the Bois to look at the beautiful child in white—white fur coat, white gaiters, and followed by a white pom—was a more refined instrument than Philibert.

"She filtered experience through a finer sieve. She had a steadier hand. Hers was the great advantage of being able to wait for her amusement and her effects. She was economical of her material. Philibert was afraid of running through the whole of experience and exhausting too soon the resources of life. Bianca was not afraid of anything, not even of being bored. She meted out pleasure with deliberation. She calculated her

capital with fine precision, she measured the future
with a centimetre rule, and poured out sensation
into a spoon, sipping it slowly."

When lifted from the context, Bianca and Philibert seem to border on the melodramatic, but it is
the triumph of Miss Borden's art that in the woof
of the story they are not only convincing but
inevitable. One feels the quality of Bianca's charm
even when she drifts into the hotel at Biarritz,
a shabby, drug-racked old woman. It is Jane, not
they, who seems exaggerated as the story closes
in that weather-beaten gray house in St. Mary's
Plains where Grandmother Forbes used to sit in
her armchair by the living-room window and nod
over the top of her spectacles to her acquaintances
who passed in the street.

Three Pilgrims and a Tinker, in many respects
Miss Borden's most delightful book, is a study in
contrasts of another sort. Marion Dawnay, although she was an Englishwoman, was a sunny,
exotic cosmopolitan, drifting from pleasure to
pleasure, following the sun from Paris to Florence,
to Rome, wherever fancy dictated, passively
avoiding tiresome things like responsibilities or
solemn people, idling in the enjoyment of the
moment. She was set down by a casual fate in the
English midlands. Marion hated the blustering
cold midlands, the sodden fields, the flooded
brooks, the ugly houses whose chief attractions
were their hot baths. She hated the savage delight

of her husband and neighbours in racing against the wind and sleet, following the hounds in delirious pursuit of the red fox; but the country got her, the hunt got her finally. As one watches Marion succumb to the fascination of the hunt, one comes to an understanding of the harsh, rich, damp, sodden charm of middle England. One can smell and feel and savour the ecstasy of a furious ride with the clouds streaming overhead, and afterward the contentment of tea before the bright fire at home, with a hot bath as the climax of a perfect day.

Miss Borden knows her midlands. Much of her time is spent in Leicestershire, where her husband has stood for Parliament in a mining and agricultural constituency. She knows far more of it than the hunting set, for while that is an exclusive and complete world in itself, there are many other aspects. One cannot live in this section of England, she thinks, without becoming aware of the revolutionary social forces that are at work. Life is indeed a serious business since the war, and it is impossible not to take a keen interest in political and industrial problems. There is no greater contrast, she finds, between the outlook of the average Englishwoman of the middle or upper classes and that of her prototype in America, because the American women, even the mass of American men, find little to interest them in politics.

Another phase of life in the midlands upon

which Miss Borden touches lightly in *Three Pilgrims and a Tinker*, she develops in the theme of a later novel, *Jericho Sands*. With much the same setting as *Three Pilgrims and a Tinker*, Miss Borden finds her story in a native drama. All the elements of this gallant and pitiful tale are rooted, age-old, in the land itself. Priscilla Brampton's fox-hunting father who rode to the hounds four days and spent the others about his stables; her gentle, shabby lady mother who went flatfooted along the highroads scattering tracts, calling the tramps and itinerant workmen to Jesus Christ; Simon, her beautiful, evangelical young husband, torn between his passion for her and his passion for his God; last of all, Crab Willing, the keen, cool, hard-living heir of Jericho Sands, officer, big-game hunter, good rider, excellent shot, the much-desired guest at country parties, booked weeks in advance, in fact, the most perfect and self-sufficient flower of English civilization. From this triangle, Miss Borden builds a story of remarkable psychological insight and power, a story in which one is brought to understand and sympathize with each of the three who unwillingly wrecked the others.

Although most of Miss Borden's novels and short stories are about people of the social order in which she herself lives, her range is not bounded by class. Several of the most effective tales in the collection, *Four o'Clock*, are concerned with poor unfortunates at the bottom of the scale.

The squinting, club-footed little maid-of-all-work who wanted a doll, in "Beauty," and the delicatessen poet who attained respectability for an hour in "An Accident on the Quai Voltaire," are creations fully as authentic as the lion-hunting hostess, or the gentlewoman who stood by, in "Tapestry Needlework." In "No Verdict," the tale of a pitiful young druggist's clerk, who lacked the courage to drink the poison that his sweetheart left and sat through the murder trial shivering with self-reproach, more afraid of life than death, she reaches a high level of restraint and beauty. This story is the only fictional propaganda that Miss Borden has ever written. The English law which provides the death penalty for the survivor of a suicide pact first attracted her interest years ago when she followed a case in which the injustice of the law was strikingly evident. When the defendant, a survivor of a suicide pact, was tried the first time, the judge postponed the trial, at the second trial he was sentenced to be tried a third time, but he died in prison from the strain of it. Brigadier General Spears was also interested, and some time ago—he was then an M. P.—he introduced a bill into the House of Commons to amend the suicide-pact law. The bill has had a first reading and there is hope that it will become a law.

Miss Borden does not believe in capital punishment in any case, although she thinks that the English law should discriminate between a man who is sincerely depressed and wants to die and between the person who so influences another to the extent that he or she commits suicide. Where two helpless people are encumbering the earth and feel it, as in the story "No Verdict," there is no happiness for them—they cannot make a living, and in such a case it is surely the height of agonizing irony to hang a man because he failed to die. "I don't think suicide is a crime," she says. "We had no choice about being born, and we have a right to die."

Miss Borden spent much time at Old Bailey while she was writing this story, and her contact with the grimmest of English courts strengthened her belief in the unjustifiability of capital punishment. "We have jurisdiction only over this earth," she maintains. "If one goes beyond judgment for this life, one goes beyond one's limit of judgment. The law has to protect society but has nothing to do with our immortal souls."

"No Verdict" was also the occasion of one of those queer trials for libel in which Englishmen of leisure indulge. It seems that one of the minor characters in the story, called in the American edition, Lady Pym-Dymock, felt that youth had flown, that life was not as amusing as it used to be, and incidentally that her husband was a bore. Miss Borden gave this casual spectator at the trial a combination of typical English names which she believed were of her own invention. Unfortunately, the names did belong to a real lady

whose husband objected to being labelled tiresome, so he asked the courts for proper damages.

Another of the stories in *Four o'Clock* has a
history. "Miss Bateman and the Medium" so
interested the Psychical Research Society of
London that she was asked to let its members
have a pen or paper weight or some object that
had been with her manuscript. They plan to give it
to a medium in the hope of discovering whether
any mental currents emanate from the object, and
by this means determine whether or not the
subconscious currents of a mind when it becomes
overheated by the imagination are transferred
to objects in the immediate vicinity. The story
itself is concerned with the helplessness of a distinguished, fastidious novelist, so obsessed with
a set of thoroughly distasteful and uncontrollable
characters that she began to wonder if they really
had an independent existence and a right to live
lives of their own.

How Miss Borden finds the time to do the
amount and quality of work that have come from
her pen within the last seven or eight years is a
mystery to those who are familiar with her social
and political activities. The author of five published novels, a book of short stories, and a sixth
now in the hands of her publishers, she manages
to supervise the training of her four children, to
give her husband active support in his political
career, and to be one of the most smartly dressed
and active of London's hostesses. She has no

hobbies because she finds life so extraordinarily full that there has been no opportunity for them. One of her regrets is that she did not study science, and she is hoping at this late date to find time to begin the study of higher mathematics. Always she is at work on a book or a story. When one is finished, she is restless until another is begun.

When in town, Miss Borden lives in one of the most beautiful old houses in London, a house designed by Lutyens in Little College Street, just behind Westminster Abbey and well within the sound of Big Ben. The great hallway and main staircase are of veined, cream-coloured marble, and the library is finished in the beautiful, natural panelling for which many old English houses are famous. The floor of the dining room is made of squares of polished steel that gleam like silver. On this stands a dining table made of a solid slab of green marble, flanked by chairs of a soft yellow decorated with delightful little red flowers. This gracious old house with its daring modern touches is a perfect setting for Miss Borden's sophisticated and by no means colourless personality. Here she gathers about her the most brilliant members of London's diplomatic and artistic world. At a recent musicale in the drawing-room on Little College Street, Miss Borden's sister, the wife of the Croatian violinist, Zlatko Balakovic, wore an embroidered satin gown which her mother had bought in Paris for her own trousseau forty years ago.

But London claims comparatively little of Miss Borden's time. Often she is in Leicestershire. Last summer she and the General took an old castle in the Burgundian Mountains in the heart of a forest where their chief amusement was the ancient French sport of hunting the wild boar.

Miss Borden's children are sturdy little sportsmen, happiest when out of doors. While there are no definite portraits of them in *Three Pilgrims and a Tinker*, no one could have written that tender and exquisite story of Jill and Babs and greedy little Biddy without having loved and lived and played with babies of one's own. There are too few children in Miss Borden's stories. Nowhere in her work does one find displayed to better advantage the subtle delicacies and cool restrained brilliance of her style.

EDWARD A. WILSON

EDWARD A. WILSON

A Sand-dune Sailor

EDWARD A. WILSON, whose woodcuts of rollicking tars are the delight of his brother craftsmen
as well as all lovers of the days of wooden ships,
has never been a deep-sea sailor, but he grew up
in the tradition of the sea. Born in Glasgow, where
he could watch the tall spars of the North Sea
fishing fleet riding in the harbour, Wilson moved
as a little boy to Rotterdam. His father, who was
in the shipping business, knew all the captains on
the stately square-riggers in the harbour. Every
evening that the boy and his father were not dining aboard ship, there were captains at home for
dinner, slow, dignified captains with white beards,
jolly, red-faced captains who told great stories to
little boys, captains of all kinds and shapes and
sizes, but all with a present in their pockets, some
trinket from a far-away port that filled the child
with a wanderlust he has never outgrown.

Later the family moved to Chicago, and for
seventeen years, the boy was away from salt
water. Wilson earned his living during the day
by such jobs as figuring profits in a wholesale
grocery business. At night he studied at the Art

Institute, but every once in a while he broke away
to sail the Great Lakes in lumber freighters and
schooners. His first art job was at five dollars a
week, but he soon did a prize poster for an electri-
cal show, then posters for several motor-boat
shows, and later illustrations for those alluring
railroad and steamship booklets that tempt the
cautious stay-at-home to travel.

After spending two years working with Howard
Pyle and his students at Wilmington, Delaware,
painting shipwrecks and marines, Wilson settled
down on Cape Cod with a house, a large studio, a
press for printing woodcuts, a wife, two children,
and plenty of sea and weather. Here he has added
yearly to his reputation until he has become known
as one of the finest woodcut artists in America.

Several years ago, Wilson illustrated his first
book, *Iron Men and Wooden Ships*, a collection of
deep-sea chanties for which he designed the gay
boards, the vivid green labels, the title page, all
the decorations, and four-colour woodcuts which
made it one of the most alluring of sea books. Last
year he did another rollicking volume, *Full and By*,
an anthology of drinking songs of all ages. His
first editions are eagerly sought, both by the artist and the collector, and his sailors have been
called the happiest of all tributes to the age of
wooden ships.

Indeed, the sea is so much a part of Wilson's
life that he is not content long away from it. On
Cape Cod he is called the sand-dune sailor because

his home is a veritable ship ashore. The house is an old one set back about a quarter of a mile from the sea in one of those snug little valleys that old salts always choose when they finally come to harbour. Once it belonged to a pirate, and the Wilsons cherish the hope that one of the beams in the barn is a relic of the wreck of the pirate Bellamy in 1717. Many of the neighbours still have pieces of eight salvaged from that occasion.

The old white barn which, in true New England style, was larger than the house Mr. Wilson moved up into the foreground, connected it with the house by a high picket fence and turned it into a studio. In one of the horse stalls he parks his car. The loft he has converted into a guest room by enclosing it with a rope railing, a fireplace has been built into one end, and he has as comfortable and picturesque a studio as one could well imagine. There he has gathered around him all the tools of his work, even to the Washington hand press now used for proving wood blocks.

All summer long the Wilsons live in their "stationary ship," and often, late into the fall, the artist may be seen walking the beach with the lifeguards, or combing the coasts for ship models and books and prints of the sea.

SIR HUGH CLIFFORD

MAHLEN BLAINE

SIR HUGH CLIFFORD

An Englishman in the Orient

OF THOSE who have been able to recreate in
words the magic of the inland seas, the jungle
trails, and wide lazy rivers of the Malay peninsula,
Joseph Conrad and Sir Hugh Clifford stand supreme, Conrad because of the glamour with which
his genius touches whatever he chose to write,
and Sir Hugh Clifford because, in addition to his
fine sense of the values of English prose, he knows
Malaya, the old regenerate Malaya of barbaric
splendour, with an intimacy that is given to few
white men.

Although his life has been spent in establishing
that efficient English order which is converting
the far corners of the East into prosaic communi-
ties as safe as London suburbs, Sir Hugh gives
many a pensive thought to those adventurous
days when he, in his high-hearted twenties, wore
a silk sarong and lived at the court of an inland
sultan for months at a time without seeing a white
face. To read any of his stories is to read a chapter
of his biography, because all of them are based on
incidents that happened to him or came to his
knowledge in carrying on the daily job, or reflect

165

some common aspect of the life around him. To call them fiction when they are in the main a record of fact seemed to him a kind of imposture.

To the seventeen-year-old boy straight from Sandhurst, determined to better the illustrious record of his father the Major General with V. C., K. C. M. G., and C. B. after his name, the East held a glamour and a fascination that never palled for the man. From the moment that he caught his first whiff of Asia as the P. & O. steamer approached Ceylon, and saw the palm fronds skirting the shore, the white, sun-baked streets, the ox-carts, the bright, clamouring crowds, and sniffed the warm, moist smell of ripe fruit, he was filled with a vivid delight.

After three years of intensive application to the language, the bookkeeping, and such other details of government as the young Civil Service cadets are supposed to absorb, Sir Hugh had a marvellous bit of luck. A hard-pressed colonial governor sent him on a special mission to the Sultan of Pahang, a large state on the Eastern seaboard, because, as he modestly explains, there were no senior men with the necessary qualifications who could be spared for so long a period. So the boy, not yet twenty, set out on the long overland journey over the mountains and through the jungles peopled only by wild animals and the equally wild Sakai tribesmen, and returned three months later bearing in triumph to Singapore a treaty surrendering the Sultan's foreign relations into the hands

of the British government. His crossing of the
jungle-clad mountains Sir Hugh records in that
tale of the lone-hand raid of Kŭlop Sŭmbing which
is the literary father of Eugene O'Neill's equally
powerful *Emperor Jones*. The steep ascents that
had to be scaled by means of roots and slender
saplings, the bare drumming grounds of the magnificent argus pheasants who nightly strut and
dance but are rarely seen by human eyes, the
blurred blue-gray foliage pierced by splotches of
sunlight on the river, he saw them when his young
imagination was avid of impressions.

And the Sultan's court at which he resided for
nearly two years as the first British Agent was
almost an exact counterpart to the feudal king-
doms of mediæval Europe. Many of his stories
have as their setting just such a Sultan's court
as the one at which he spent his novitiate. A long
string of ramshackle buildings surrounded by a
split bamboo fence was generally the Sultan's
palace. The largest thatched house in the middle
contained His Majesty's own apartments, that
of his favourite concubine, and the other ladies
of the court. Here he stayed in seclusion for days
at a time, gambling, or loafing with his women.
It was difficult to find him, and for months at a
time, when the resident wished to see him on
unpleasant business, or any boring details of official life seemed about to be thrust upon him,
the attendants sent word that "His Majesty
sleepeth." Between the King's young men, a

swaggering bodyguard of bravely silk-decked
young warriors, and the King's women, who were
supposed to live in celibacy awaiting the favour
of their monarch, there were constant intrigues
which involved diabolical tortures and sudden
death.

In *A Prince of Malaya*, the tragic story of
"Sally," the King's heir, who was sent to England
at an early age, educated at Oxford, converted
into a conventional young Englishman, and then
returned to the squalor and conflicting customs of
his native state, one gets an intimate view of life
as it was lived in Malaya at the beginning of the
white man's rule. Minah and her man the leper,
the two little runaway Mohammedan girls, and
most of the characters in *The Further Side of
Silence*, and *Malayan Monochromes*, were familiar
people in his district, all of their stories he had
seen or had been told by brother officers of the
Civil Service in those rare moments when they
talk to each other about the unending puzzle of the
Oriental mind.

From that first mission to the Sultan of Pahang,
Sir Hugh Clifford climbed steadily upward. In
1894, he was Commissioner to the Cocos Keeling
Islands, those sunny atolls in the Indian Ocean
whose nearest neighbour is Sumatra, seven hundred miles away. In 1903, he became Colonial
Secretary of Tobago and Trinidad, which have
increased mightily in population since Tobago
was Robinson Crusoe's island home. After acting

as Colonial Secretary to Ceylon, he was made
Governor of the Gold Coast, in 1912, and now
has returned to the Ceylon, as its Colonial Governor.

But Malaya, his first love, has always retained
the strongest hold upon Sir Hugh's imagination.
With Sir Frank Swettenham, he compiled a dic-
tionary of the Malay languages and made a Malay
translation of the penal code, and Malayan scenes
and peoples have given him the material for all
of his stories. Through many of them runs a
wistfulness for the good old days when he was
young and eager for adventure and the East was
unregenerate. "Trusty and Well-Beloved," in
Malayan Monochromes, is one of the most poignant
laments for the glamour of a lost youth that one
can find in English prose. When Sir Philip Hanbury-Erskine, G. C. B., G. C. M. G., looked out
on the sleeping capital of the kingdom to which
he had been elevated that day, the goal of a hard-
working, practical man who had had little time
for dreaming and felt suddenly a great weariness,
a nostalgia for the bazaars, the scent of spice
and garlic and fruit, the brushing of shoulders with
the native ant heap of voluptuous humanity, when
he left his official self and his official responsibilities in the Governor's mansion with his
pajamas and slipped over the porch rail in native
costume to revisit the cafés and alleyways and old
familiar haunts of the faithful which had remained
unchanged for a quarter of a century, Sir Hugh

is writing of himself. He may not have kicked off his shoes and with his own bare feet puddled the dust of the road, but his spirit went adventuring with Sir Philip Hanbury-Erskine when His Excellency the Governor kicked over the traces and reverted to his youth.

WALTER JACK DUNCAN

Walter Jack Duncan

WALTER JACK DUNCAN

Wizard of Pen and Ink

IT IS the happy illustrator whose brush so perfectly visualizes the author's intent that his illustrations become as vital a part of the story as the
text itself. He is a creator who shares equally with
the author in the making of beautiful books, but to
the reader he is indefinite. The author is a familiar
figure. His picture, and that of his wife and children, his home, and his dog, appear again and again
in the literary journals. One knows what he likes
for breakfast, what are his favourite sports and
pet aversions, and all the intimate little details
that create a friendly personality. But the illustrator remains a disembodied pen.

No one who keeps volumes of Christopher
Morley's books on his bedside shelf can be insensible to the charm of Walter Duncan's pen drawings in *Pipefuls*, *Plum Pudding*, and *Tales from a
Rolltop Desk*. Duncan, with his mastery of line and
fecund imagination, visualizes as if they were a part
of his own experience Morley's city squares and
railway stations, docks and country lanes, his
wistful dogs, his fishermen, and all the company
that throng his pages.

Although he is one of the foremost illustrators in New York and has lived for a long time not many steps around the corner from the old Brevoort, he is in reality one of those Hoosiers who helped to make Indianapolis famous. He and his chum, Bob Holliday, more formally known among the literati as Robert Cortes Holliday, were playing with the Penrods of their neighbourhood in the back yards and alleys of the half-grown city while Tarkington was a college boy writing plays for school dramatics, and James Whitcomb Riley, not yet famous, was writing some of his best poems. Life had a pleasant expansiveness. It was before the era of butlers. When Mother wanted to go down town, the Negro who mowed the lawns, kept the furnace, and did odd jobs around the house, hitched up the horses and acted as coachman. There were spacious back yards and barns to play in, and the old Arsenal was a favourite stamping ground. When they had finished high school, Duncan and Holliday came to New York and shared the proverbial garret while they studied art at the Art Students' League. This particular garret was on Broome Street, and there are many amusing glimpses of it in Mr. Holliday's *Broome Street Straws*. The boys became pupils of the great John H. Twachtman, the brusque little man with graying bangs and a mephistophelian manner, whom his fellow artists pronounced the greatest of American landscape artists.

Their first exhibit was a magic event. The Double-

day, Page Book Shop on Fifth Avenue displayed
a number of their poster drawings, and as a result
Chapin, the art editor of *Century Magazine*, offered
to use three drawings of each in his next issue.
What an interminable time it seemed before publication date. Almost every evening the boys walked
by the Century Company building, just to make
sure that it hadn't burned down or been wrecked
during the day. When the magazine finally came
out, they rushed to the stand and bought probably
the first two copies that left the press. But what
was their grief to discover that the names had been
switched. Holliday's drawings were credited to
Duncan, and Duncan's to Holliday. Soon afterward, Duncan got a commission in New York,
but it was not his first, for he had already done
illustrations for two books. The first was a volume
written by a young uncle, a remarkable boy who,
when he died at the age of fourteen, was a feature-
story writer on one of the large Philadelphia dail-
ies. The book was the record of the boy's travels
with his father, Walter Duncan's grandfather,
John Jack, the first American actor to conduct an
American troupe around the world. John Jack
was a famous Falstaff, and Riley always insisted
that he was the greatest actor of the part in
America, although his Sir Anthony Absolute was
equally well known, sharing honours for many
seasons with Jefferson's Bob Acres in *The Rivals*.
Mr. Duncan's connection with the stage goes
farther back than this grandfather, for his great-

grandfather was John Roland Reed, known to the Philadelphia theatres for seventy years. Roland Reed, his son, was a famous comedian, whose daughter, Florence Reed, has in turn made a name in the theatre. Duncan's mother, Rosalie Jack, made her first appearance on the stage at the age of six months, and when she was a few years older played Minna in Joseph Jefferson's *Rip Van Winkle*. She also played with Booth, McCullough, and Forrest. Altogether, it was a stimulating household for a boy with imagination. Mr. Duncan consequently has a fondness for the theatre, and has in his studio an interesting collection of autographed photographs of actor friends.

In addition to illustrating books, Mr. Duncan has done work for many of the leading magazines. *Scribner's* sent him to London in 1905 for a set of drawings, and *Harper's* has sent him to Canada and to the Kentucky mountains, where he drew the descendants of Daniel Boone and his pioneers living under the same conditions that their ancestors found when they first surged across the mountains.

A signal recognition of Duncan's work as an illustrator came during the war when he was chosen by the National Committee, headed by Charles Dana Gibson, as one of the eight official artists who accompanied the A. E. F. He was given a roving commission as a captain in the engineering corps, and managed to record in his sketches five major operations.

Pen drawing is Mr. Duncan's favourite medium, especially for book illustration. "An illustration drawn in line with a pen and ink, and in the manner that types were originally designed is," he says, "naturally enough, in perfect keeping with the text, and with it sparkles enchantingly against its sunny background of white paper. Simple, logical, cheap, autographic, beautiful, say what you will, as a vehicle for the practical illustration it is unique and beyond compare, the prince of mediums."

HAROLD MacGRATH

HAROLD MACGRATH

Minky Moy, Poppies, and Pussy Willows

HAROLD MACGRATH'S studio, where he concocts best sellers about the adventures of the fair heroine en route to the altar, is his garden. And one who sees it can readily understand why he sometimes dips his pen into rainbows instead of sober ink. It is a garden made to dream in. There is nothing formal, no suggestion of the Italian renaissance or the landscape architect, neither is it prim and old-fashioned, although there are hollyhocks and roses. Through paths that wind between poppy beds, one comes to a pool, rock-edged, reflecting pussy willows, and across a little wooden bridge is a bit of lawn with a hammock, easy chairs, a sundial, and a rough stone seat in the shade.

Here Mr. MacGrath sits and dreams out his romances, although the actual work of writing them is done on his time-worn Remington indoors. Here Minky Moy rolls in the grass and barks at the tenants of the bird house or the goldfish in the pool. Minky Moy is the author's favourite pet. Nominally she is Mrs. MacGrath's, but virtually she is his.

The dog is about as big as her master's scarf pin.

177

Her tongue is like a little piece of narrow pink ribbon. She is successor to Fritz, a dachshund from the royal Bavarian kennels, used by the MacGraths as a passport through the German Empire some years before the war.

But Minky doesn't like this writing business. She is a veteran fisherman, like her master, and occasionally drags up a mouthful of earthworms to remind him of the sport. She loves the bait herself when her diminutive palate is jaded by Far Western dog biscuits, but she always brings them to her best friend first. In the morning, she brings him a consignment from the garden, laying them on the floor beside the mantel under the miniature autographed bust of Mark Twain, which jostles a like replica of Irvin Cobb there. Then she helps the boss dress, taking one shoe to the bathroom and another downstairs, and tying his trousers diligently into knots. He would never think of going fishing without her.

Mr. MacGrath is a great adventurer, and his stories are all based upon some fact of his own experiences in the four corners of the world. In his quiet garden, he works over material gathered in the strange places that he has seen—Europe, Africa, Asia, the China Seas. He incorporates in his stories the bite of a typhoon, the swinging monotony of endless cabins, the burning ghats of Benares, the dance halls of Sumatra, the gardens of the Mikado. A very small incident will often start a story. *Drums of Jeopardy* grew from an emerald that he once saw on the Ponte Vecchio, Florence, a pendant as large as a half dollar and about half an inch thick. Day after day, on the way to the Pitti Galleria, MacGrath stopped at the window to look at the beautiful stone. Jewels have a strong fascination for him, not to wear but to feast his eyes upon, to touch and play with. When he was in Delhi, he haunted the Chandu Chowk, the Maiden Lane of all India, and held in his hands many fabulous pink pearls, emeralds, pigeon-blood rubies, and sapphires.

Harold MacGrath, who is now nearing fifty, has been writing steadily for the last thirty years, starting as a cub reporter on the Syracuse *Herald* at eighteen. When twenty-eight, he wrote his first novel, and since then has written, perhaps, more best sellers than any of his contemporaries. He is now ranked among the seven best-selling novelists of the United States. In an old scrapbook he has kept much of the verses and clever nonsense that he used to turn out for his column in the *Herald*. It is not all collected, but there are miles and miles of it. An estimate of his works runs well above a million printed words.

In the afternoons, Mr. MacGrath deserts his garden studio and goes to the movies. He is a great "movie hound," in spite of his first unfortunate experience with the films. "The first movie I ever saw," he says, "was at Keith's, New York, after an evening cloistered with the Friars or gambolling with the Lambs. Breakfast was two quarts of strawberries and some champagne. Film ran backwards. It was a horse race. I nearly swore off then, but saw the film right end to the next time, and that was long before the Eighteenth Amendment." Now he never misses a picture of promising title.

In the summer, when they are not wandering around the world, the writer, Mrs. MacGrath, and Minky Moy fish for bass at Cape Vincent, New York. But after Labour Day he comes back to his work and the autumn beauty of his garden.

SAX ROHMER

SAX ROHMER

And the Art of Making Villains

SAX ROHMER, who has created more numerous
and fascinating villains than anyone since Gilbert
and Sullivan, admits that this art of thrill-making
was not entirely a natural gift. It was developed
by a series of experiments with various other
professions, each of which gave him some special
bit of knowledge or ingenious idea for the alluring
black magic of his stories. From *Dr. Fu-Manchu*
to *Yellow Shadows*, Rohmer has flashed against
richly exotic backgrounds such diabolically ingenious and irresistible villains as one trusts this
world has never seen.

Sax Rohmer's own dizzy career has been a series
of valiant attacks on fortune and hasty retreats
when he met her face to face. He has always intended to be an author, and although he assures
a biographer that he wrote nothing worthy of mention before the age of four, his first serious work,
"The Man in the White Hat," was written sometime during his early school days. The boy had
fallen under the spell of Mark Twain, and this
story was the outcome. It was rejected by every
periodical published in Great Britain.

At the age of nineteen, young Sax had one wall of his den papered with a design made up of editorial regrets. By this time, there were ten or a dozen short stories which had travelled separately over the entire United Kingdom. Forced to the conclusion that editors were not reading his stories the youthful author hit upon the scheme of affecting writing paper of unusual colour and envelopes of extraordinary size. Nothing happened. Finally, two stories were accepted within twenty-four hours of each other. One editor asked Rohmer to call, and suggested that he do a series of stories dealing with the same character. The shock was nearly fatal. The boy immediately left England and wrote no more for five or six years. He studied in several art schools with the intention of becoming a black-and-white artist, although he met with nothing but discouragement. Being young, failure stimulated him immensely. He worked day and night and bombarded the illustrated press with drawings. Then one day *Judy* accepted a drawing and asked him to call. From that day to this, he has done no more drawings.

Abandoning art, Rohmer converted a "studio" into a rehearsal theatre and, with three partners, prepared a one-act play for the variety stage. They finally secured a "trial week," but the playlet "got the hook," and thus closed this dramatic episode.

The next plunge was into musical composition, but the music publishers were not impressed.

With lyrics and light concert numbers, however, Rohmer had fair success. A friend introduced him to a famous concert artist, for whom he immediately wrote a character song which the artist resolutely declined to sing. Spurred to renewed efforts, he wrote others, and finally the artist tried one with success. Things went swimmingly. One or two musical compositions were published. Then came the end. The artist offered him a contract, and a music publisher in London requested him to join his staff.

Immediately, Rohmer got into touch with a tramp skipper and was arranging a voyage to South America when a long-missing friend, a medical student, turned up with a scheme for putting a new kind of moth ball on the market. After feverish periods of chemical activity, the two young promoters were forced to admit that the moth balls failed to attract. In an idle moment, Rohmer rewrote an old story which elicited from a publisher a proposition to continue the series indefinitely. It was a crucial moment. A steamer carrying general cargo was leaving the Thames for Spanish ports on the following morning. Rohmer resisted the temptation and stayed in London to complete his first series. Since then, other pursuits, no matter how alluring, have failed to entice him away from his most fascinating of occupations, the art of making villains.

KATHARINE von DOMBROWSKI

Lather Dombrowski

KATHARINE VON DOMBROWSKI

Her Adventures among Animals

FROM the earliest beginning, Katharine von Dombrowski was one of those whose restless feet answer the call of the red gods to the earth's far corners. Her Hungarian father, Ludwig Schoenberger, and her Bohemian mother spent most of the year travelling, but the child called home either Vienna or a pleasant country house in Abbazzia on the southern coast of the Adriatic Sea. The father was a connoisseur and collector of art, so the little girl was brought up in the famous galleries of Europe and fed daily on art history. But for pictures she cared not at all. Her greatest delight was animals—cats, all of the nursery pets, and especially horses. When she began to draw with chalk on the nursery floor, the nurse and the governess were always pictured on horseback, no difference how uncomfortable they actually might have been on the spirited mounts she gave them. Another game was to put animals' heads on human bodies, a talent which later brought her international fame.

At fourteen, Katharine's first book of drawings was published, and by the time it appeared a year later in England the little girl was a child phenom-

enon, petted and interviewed and generally exhibited like the most spectacular sideshow at a
circus. Fortunately, all the fuss neither bothered
nor impressed her, for she was interested only in
horses and spent the time happily riding or playing about the stables. She was equally unim-
pressed by the stern warning of the German
artist, Max Liebermann, who thought it would
be much better if she spent her time studying art
instead of horses. Indeed, most of the leading
artists in Berlin were discouraging, because the
child did not draw from life, and it was against
all tradition to draw well without a model. The
unexpected praise of the great Adolph Menzel,
who met Katharine shortly before his death and
predicted for her a fine artistic future, was her
greatest pride, especially because Menzel was
famous for his incivility and his generally low opinion of women as artists.

With her marriage to Frank Olshausen, a
member of the German Diplomatic Service,
Katharine Schoenberger began a nomadic life in
South America that was to be the happiest as well
as the most vivid and adventurous period of her
career. Accompanying her husband to his posts
in Argentine, Paraguay, south and north Brazil,
she penetrated with him into the little-known
interior of the continent, hunting, collecting,
studying the folklore of the Indians, and especially
the animal life of the forests. They were strenuous
days, often full of danger, always full of new

experiences. Occasionally, they stumbled upon conditions that filled them with impotent sadness because of their helplessness to interfere. One such experience was a visit to a lonely and primitive little settlement of European colonists who made a practice of hunting the Indians across the Iguazú River like game, burning their huts and destroying their property as if they were dangerous wild animals. These Indians, the Botocudos, were the only hostile tribe in the country, and the colonists shrugged their shoulders to all objections. Two years after this visit, the Botocudos attacked and destroyed the settlement.

At their special request Katharine Olshausen and her husband were sent to Pará in north Brazil, a post feared and avoided by everyone in the service. It was "The Green Hell," the wonderful Amazon territory with its giant river, its blight of yellow fever and untamed wilderness. After taking her nine-months-old baby to her parents in Europe, Katharine joined her husband at Pará. Together they took many journeys of exploration up the Amazon, its tributary rivers and dead streams. Once they penetrated to the foot of the Peruvian Andes, crossing the greater part of the continent. On this trip, Katharine made her most precious collections, including a new specimen of the smallest known monkey which she found hidden under the hair of an Indian girl.

Just before the outbreak of the war, Katharine

went to Cameroon, a German colony in West
Africa, where she hunted elephant. Although she
did not bring back any trophies of the gun, she
found the opportunities for which she had come,
the chance to study elephants at close range.
Several times she had the good fortune to watch
them from as near as fifteen feet. The African
elephant, which she thinks much more intelligent
and interesting than his Indian brother, furnished
her with the subjects for several of her most remarkable etchings of animals in caricature. A dry-
point of an elephant and a swaggering, truculent
little monkey at fists' points has attracted much
attention at exhibitions.

One trophy of the hunt which was much rarer
than an elephant was a huge giant scorpion which
she presented to the Hagenbeck's celebrated
zoölogical garden in Hamburg. While in Cameroon
the Baroness started a chameleon farm in two
large open cases, each with a shrub in the centre.
She had more than thirty specimens of fierce
double-horned *chamaeleon montium*, and so great
was her success that she brought seven out of nine
to Europe. Other trophies which returned with
her were a mandrill and a blue-and-red-faced
baboon who developed into such a terrible huge
devil under the influence of civilization that he
had to be kept behind double gates.

While she is travelling, Katharine von Dombrowski rarely touches a pencil or a brush, relying
upon her memory to soak up and filter the essen-

tial characteristics of things seen. She believes very little in teachers and schools of art, and thinks that the best training can be gained by the mutual work and instruction of a number of artists. The advice of older artists cost her years. Discouraged by the autocratic rules which were proclaimed to govern painting, she did very few oils until a chapter in Mereschkowski's *Leonardo da Vinci* opened up to her a new vista. One evening in Buenos Aires, Katharine Olshausen was reading the chapter in which the pupils of Leonardo discuss the question whether a simple white wall could be used as an attractive artistic motive. She was so fired with the idea that she laid the book aside, got brushes and a canvas, and that same night composed a picture with a white wall dominating the scene. Two years later, on her return to Germany, she did it in larger size. It was exhibited at the Berlin International Exhibition of 1906 and was one of her greatest successes. From that time, the way was clear. It is difficult, she thinks, for the young artist to-day to steer between the many different schools of art. There is but one reliable guide, the truth as he sees it, and absolute sincerity.

The artist's second marriage, to Baron Dombrowski, gave her leisure to live entirely for her work. For eighteen years her drawings have appeared in the *Fliegende Blaetter* of Munich, and her satirical animal caricatures have also appeared in several bound volumes.

For some time the Baroness has lived in New York devoting her time chiefly to drypoints of sports and sportsmen, polo, horse shows, racing, all those sports in which one sees beautiful high-spirited animals. She is also working on a collection of hitherto uncollected Brazilian folk tales which, with her illustrations, she hopes to make a volume of genuine historical value.

THE END